BUILDING BETTER READERS

2nd Edition

A Guide to Literacy Development for SLPs

SHARI ROBERTSON

DYNAMIC RESOURCES LLC

For Merrelyn Bird Brand, who showed me the way.

For Tom, who makes the journey worthwhile.

FOREWORD

I am so privileged to have had the opportunity to travel the country to interact with you, my colleagues, through seminars and workshops related to facilitating language and literacy. From state to state, county to county, district to district, I am constantly impressed by your dedication, your energy, your amazing talent, and your true commitment to providing high quality services for every child—for every student—for every hour—of every day. You wear many hats and your plates are very full, but still you come to listen, to share, to learn, and, hopefully, to be energized and re-charged.

I am also humbled that you have been so enthusiastic and supportive of my efforts to translate the research literature into practical, clinical applications. In fact, it has been this outpouring of support that has led to the development of this resource. I have had so many requests to capture my workshops in print that I knew it was time to actually sit down and do it! So, you hold in your hands the result of our combined efforts—your support, encouragement, and suggestions and my determination to develop a truly useful clinical resource, written specifically for speech-language pathologists to help them facilitate the literacy development of the students they serve. This 2nd edition includes additional material that I have developed since BBR was first published in 2013. I am truly humbled by the continued interest in my work.

As with any construction project, we start building better readers by laying a strong foundation. Consequently, a summary of the current literature base related to literacy development is included in each chapter to support our practice. However, the primary purpose of this resource is to provide you with evidence-based, clinically-useful strategies that can be implemented immediately in your professional setting. To that end, I have included strategies for a variety of ages, abilities levels, and clinical settings. From preschool through high school, in small and large groups, in schools, homes, or clinics—and all can be modified to help you build your students into better readers and all are supported by empirical evidence.

Finally, be forewarned that this book, for better or worse, is an extension of me. You will find that it is written in first person language—as if you and I were having a personal conversation about language and literacy. As such, depending on which part of the resource you are reading, you may find me standing on a soapbox, telling personal stories, or infusing my own personal, and admittedly often lame, attempts at humor. But, more than anything, I hope that I have conveyed my passion for the unique role we can play in facilitating literacy as well as my admiration for you—my colleagues who make it happen. This is the resource book I wish had had when I was a school-based SLP. I truly hope you find it helpful in supporting your on-going efforts to provide the best intervention possible—for every child—for every student—for every hour—of every day. I am honored to be your colleague.

You are always welcome to contact me with your thoughts and comments at shari.robertson@iup.edu.

Shari

Building Better Readers

TABLE OF CONTENTS

Chapter 1
INTRODUCTION..1

What SLPs Know About Reading	4
The Components of Language and Literacy	6
Literacy and Children with Communicative Disorders	10
Put Reading First	11
How This Book Works	12
INTRODUCTION RESOURCES	13

Chapter 2
PHONEMIC AWARENESS...21

Strategies for Building Phonemic Awareness	27
Books! Books! Books!	29
Songs! Songs! Songs!	33
Head or Toe?	36
Pack It Up!	37
Throw it Out the Window	38
Happy Hands	39
Head, Shoulders, Knees, and Toes	40
Sound Train	41
Picture Pieces	42
Box It Up	44
Jump Frog, Jump!	46
I Know Something/Someone	47
Block Activities	49
Linking Phonemic Awareness and Spelling	52
PHONEMIC AWARENESS RESOURCES	55

Building Better Readers

Chapter 3
PHONICS..75

Phonics and Language Development — 77

PHONICS RESOURCES — 81

Chapter 4
READING FLUENCY..85

The Components of Reading Fluency — 87
Reading Fluency and Pragmatics — 88
The Importance of Prosody — 88
Evaluating Reading Fluency — 89
Facilitating Reading Fluency — 89
Strategies for Building Reading Fluency — 91
- Repeated Oral Readings — 93
- Model Fluent Reading — 94
- Progressive Stories — 95
- Understanding Sentence Stress — 96
- Fun with Sentence Stress — 97
- Poetry (and Punctuation) — 100
- Songs and Chants — 102
- Choral Reading and Duet Reading — 104
- Partner Practice — 105
- Books on Tape — 106
- You Oughta Be in Pictures! — 107

READING FLUENCY RESOURCES — 109

Chapter 5
VOCABULARY..121

Word Consciousness	**124**
Typical Vocabulary Development	**124**
Classifying Vocabulary	**125**
Vocabulary Sets	**126**
What Does it Mean to "Know" a Word?	**127**
Children with Vocabulary Deficits	**129**
Strategies for Building Vocabulary	**131**
Indirect Vocabulary Development	**133**
Talking/Engaging in Oral Conversations	134
Reading Aloud	135
Independent Reading	137
Using Books to Support Vocabulary Development	138
Words of the Week	141
Vocabulary Development Via Direct Instruction	**145**
Four Square	146
Pick Six	148
Concept Map	149
SEEP	150
Brace Map	151
Alike/Different	152
Word Sorts	155
Dump and Clump	158
Picture It!	159
Imagine a Word	161
Commonyms	162
Hink-Pinks	164

Building Better Readers

Word Ladders	166
Word Strings/Word Trains	167
Don't Say It! (Taboo)	169
Scattergories	171
Analogies	172
Cinquains	173
The Match Game	176
Swat!	177
Up and Down	178
Triple Play	180
Last Person Standing	182
VOCABULARY RESOURCES	**183**

Chapter 6
READING COMPREHENSION..205

Reading with a Purpose	**207**
Active Readers	**208**
Strategies for Building Reading Comprehension	**209**
Wordless Books	211
What's My Purpose?	214
Name that Purpose	216
Here's What I Think	217
Predict-It!	219
Predict-A-Story	221
Draw-A-Story	223
Sense-O-Gram	225

Questions! Questions! Questions!	226
Top Ten Ways to Improve Your Reading	229
SQR3	230

READING COMPREHENSION RESOURCES   233

Chapter 7
THE MOTIVATION TO READ!.............................243

Eye Candy (Engaging Visual Learners)	246
For Laughing Out Loud	249
Now That's Funny!	253
Half-Baked Headlines	254
Figurative Language	255
Fractured Figurative Language!	257
Reading Circles	258

MOTIVATION TO READ RESOURCES   259

Appendix
SUPPLEMENTAL INFORMATION...........................273

Informal Assessment of Literacy Skills	275
References and Recommended Reading	277

Building Better Readers

Special Thanks To:

Diana Newman
Linda Schreiber
Cindy Earle
Brianna Robertson
Elaine Weitzman
Lynne Troyan
Sharon Jung

Who so generously shared their time, talents, advise, and expertise.

CHAPTER 1

INTRODUCTION

Introduction

For many decades, the argument over how to most effectively teach children to read seesawed between those who passionately believed that decoding was the key to reading and those who were equally passionate in their belief that language comprehension was the most critical skill for the development of literacy. This "phonics versus whole language" battle led to scores of children who were instructed using primarily one methodology or the other—often with poor results

Thankfully, a new conceptual framework, the **Simple View of Reading**, has emerged in recent years. Rather than viewing reading as an either/or choice between two opposing views, both Word Recognition and Language Comprehension are considered to be necessary components of literacy. In a nutshell, this means that successful readers must be able to recognize and decode words as well as comprehend their oral meanings. This model helps explain reading failure by students who decode well but cannot comprehend what they read as well as those who have difficulty decoding words but are able to understand material presented orally.

The emergence of the simple view of reading has been a catalyst in expanding the role of speech-language pathologists to include reading and writing. In fact, in its position statement regarding literacy, the American Speech-Language-Hearing Association (ASHA Ad Hoc Committee on Reading and Written Language Disorders, 2001) asserts that speech-language pathologists play a critical and direct role in the development of literacy for children and adolescents with communication disorders. While the notion of directly addressing written language may be somewhat new to some SLPs, most understand that reading and writing depend heavily on oral skills.

ASHA POSITION STATEMENT

• • • • • • • • • • • • • • • • • • •

Speech-Language Pathologists play a critical and direct role in the development of literacy for children and adolescents with communication disorders.

• • • • • • • • • • • • • • • • • • •

ASHA Ad Hoc Committee on Reading and Written Language Disorders, 2001

However, it is possible that, like me, you received little to no coursework related to literacy in your Master's program. Personally, it wasn't until I became interested in the development of literacy that I realized that I actually knew a LOT about it. In fact, even SLPs who have had absolutely no training in literacy know more than they think. Read on—and realize why you are already a literacy expert!

WHAT SLPS KNOW ABOUT READING

ORAL LANGUAGE IS THE KEY TO READING SUCCESS

Regardless of whether or not you were provided with specific instruction related to literacy during your university preparation, SLPs have a very strong knowledge base when it comes to reading. In fact, from the perspective of the simple view of reading, SLPs hold key and in-depth knowledge about literacy that many other professionals who work in the area of reading may not. Very few teacher education, special education, or even reading specialist programs include entire courses on normal language development. However, SLPs' comprehensive knowledge base related to oral language development is precisely what gives us an edge in terms of understanding the critical role that *oral language* plays in the development of strong reading skills.

The research is clear in demonstrating that delays in oral language development are strongly correlated with delays in literacy as children mature. Furthermore, these problems are durable and persist throughout the school years. For example:

- ❏ Children whose language skills are weak during the preschool years are at increased risk for continued language delay and for developing reading problems (Snowling, 2005).

- ❏ Among children with language delay in Kindergarten, 50% were identified with a reading disability in first or second grade (Catts et al., 2002).

- ❏ Children with weak language skills at 5½ were found to have poor reading comprehension at 8½ and 15½ (Stothard et al., 1998).

Conversely, research has proven again and again that children who have developed a strong oral language base are much more likely to learn to read more easily than students whose oral language skills are even slightly constrained.

THE LANGUAGE/LITERACY HIERARCHY

The best way that I have found to demonstrate the importance of oral language to reading and writing is by using the Language/Literacy Hierarchy. I originally developed this in response to a middle school principal who asked me—**AGAIN**—what it is that SLPs actually do and why they are important to helping children succeed in school. Out of sheer desperation, I sketched out the figure on the following page to explain how oral language (talking and listening) supports written language (reading and writing) which, in turn, supports classroom content areas. (It wasn't until much later that I realized that the language/literacy hierarchy actually does a fine job of demonstrating the importance of linguistic comprehension per the simple view of reading.)

Introduction

This hierarchy provides a visual representation of what SLPs already know. Specifically, that the critical foundation skill for academic success is ORAL language. All of the other areas related to academic success are subsets of this critical foundation skill.

I use the Language/Literacy Hierarchy whenever I am speaking to a group—large or small, professionals or parents—about literacy. Establishing the importance of the role that oral language plays in the development of written language provides the foundation upon which you can build better readers—regardless of age or ability levels.

FREE RESOURCE

You can download an animated version of the Language/Literacy Hierarchy at *www.dynamic-resources.org* or email *shari@dynamic-resource.org* and request it.

Find the narrative for the Language/Literacy Hierarchy in the *Resources* section of this chapter.

I have developed a narrative that explains the Language/Literacy Hierarchy. You can find it in the Introduction Resources section of this chapter. Please feel free to use it in any way that you choose if you find it helpful to you.

THE COMPONENTS OF LANGUAGE AND LITERACY

An SLP's knowledge base related to literacy doesn't end with the understanding of oral language development. No matter where (or when!) you were trained, you learned that language has three modes through which individuals may communicate: oral, written, and gestural. Traditionally, SLPs have concentrated more on the oral mode of communication—and do a great job at that. We are also typically very comfortable with the gestural mode. SLPs use formal and informal sign to support language development for children who are slow to talk, or those that are non-verbal, and, of course, those who are deaf or hard of hearing.

But, whether you know it or not, SLPs are also very knowledgeable about the written mode of language (reading and writing). While oral and written language are not exactly the same—reading requires some additional skills that are unique to this mode of communication—the fundamental components of oral and written language are the same. And you know these very well!

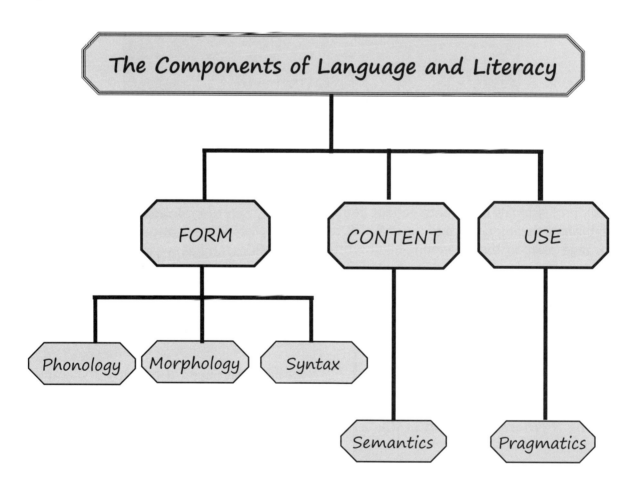

Introduction

Every SLP knows that language is made up of these three components—Form, Content, and Use. What you may not realize is that reading involves the exact same components. Let's take a look of each component in terms of how it relates to language and literacy development.

Form

Language form involves the rules we use to combine and manipulate sounds, words, and sentences to communicate our thoughts, needs, feelings, wants, and ideas. Language form, whether oral or written, involves three sub-categories: Phonology, morphology, and syntax.

> **PHONOLOGY**
> • • • • • • • • • • • • •
> *The system of rules that govern the sounds in a language.*

All languages have a set of rules for how sounds are combined. For instance, there are certain consonants, such as /ŋ/, that are never found at the beginning of English words. Similarly, there are some sounds that are found in one language that are not found in another. As an example, English does not include the "rolling r" that is found in most dialects of Spanish. Even when reading or listening to nonsense words, native speakers can pick out words that could, conceivably, be "real" words in that language versus those that could not.

For instance, in Hawaiian, all words must end with a vowel sound. So, a nonsense word such as "swit" could not be part of the Hawaiian language, although it **would** fit the phonological parameters of English. Conversely, the name of Hawaii's state fish is humuhumunukunukuapua'a—a word that definitely does not fit the phonotactic (syllable and word shape) patterns of English! (Just for fun—did you know that the entire Hawaiian phonological system includes only seven consonants? They are /h/, /k/, /l/, /m/, /n/, /p/, and of course, /w/.)

Young children's phonological systems develop rapidly. Interestingly, babies initially babble using some sounds that are not included in the language of their parents or caregivers. However, these sounds are extinguished fairly quickly so that English babies literally babble in English (that is, they use only the sounds and sound combinations found in English), French babies babble in French, and Portuguese babies babble in Portuguese! Amazingly, the phonological systems of typically developing children are essentially fully developed (in other words, they are able to produce all the sounds in their language) by the time they start Kindergarten.

However, in order to read, children must develop an ability to not only say sounds, but to segment the stream of speech into its individual components—an essential skill for the development of the sound/symbol relationship. Once children are able to understand that words are made up of sounds, they can eventually learn to represent the sound (phoneme) using a specific symbol (grapheme). Children who are unable to segment the stream of speech into individual phonemes will have a difficult time learning to read and spell (more on this later).

Building Better Readers

> **MORPHOLOGY**
> • • • • • • • • • • • • • • • •
> The system of rules that govern the internal structure of words.

The next level of language form deals with how morphemes are combined to convey meaning at the word level. For example, the root word "walk" can be modified by adding grammatical morphemes such as -s (walks), -ing (walking), or -er (walker). When assessing a developing language system, SLPs typically use the mean length of the utterances, as measured in morphemes, in a child's language sample as a measure of the development of language form and sentence complexity.

Children who struggle at the morphological level in oral language will undoubtedly also lag behind their peers in learning to read. A student's knowledge of the internal structure of words affects word recognition, spelling, and vocabulary comprehension. In addition, morphological elements give a reader cues about the meaning of a word (e.g., prefixes, tense markers, plural markers). Effective writing, not surprisingly, also requires a solid knowledge of morphology.

As we recall from our language development coursework, children typically produce single word utterances around 12 months of age. They begin to combine words around 18 months—typically using an agent-action semantic construction (roughly comparable to noun/verb). Eventually, child learn to expand the noun phrase and verb phrase in a variety of ways, through such constructs as adjectives, adverbs, conjunctions, auxiliary verbs, and superlatives.

> **SYNTAX**
> • • • • • • • • • • • • • • • •
> The system of rules that govern how sentences are constructed.

A child who does not have a good grasp of syntax in the oral mode will most likely also struggle when trying to comprehend written sentences and paragraphs. Conversely, a student who does understand grammar can forego having to figure out the syntactic form of the written passage. This allows the reader to focus their cognitive resources on constructing meaning from what is read, which is, of course, the whole purpose of reading!

CONTENT (SEMANTICS)

Introduction

Semantics deals with the meaning of language in both the oral and written modes. It would seem obvious to us that students who know more words are better readers—however, many people (educators included) don't understand how oral vocabulary can impact on reading. As demonstrated via the Language-Literacy Hierarchy, students who don't have a large *oral* vocabulary from which to draw will certainly demonstrate difficulty in comprehension of *written* passages. In other words, good readers comprehend more because they know the meanings of more words than poor readers.

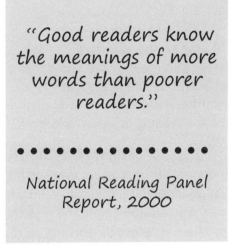

"Good readers know the meanings of more words than poorer readers."

•••••••••••••••

National Reading Panel Report, 2000

A less-robust vocabulary will also impact on a student's ability to write. Students who use incorrect or imprecise words in their written language will most likely have a harder time conveying their thoughts and ideas in this mode. Reading is, at the core, an attempt to derive or create meaning. Consequently, attention to the development of the semantic aspects of oral and written language is a critical building block for the development of literacy.

USE (PRAGMATICS)

Just like oral language, written language is a social process that requires a sender (author) and a receiver (reader). In face-to-face communication, the style of the message can be modified based on the context. For instance, in a casual conversation, the speaker may use slang, improper grammar, or even sarcasm when conveying a message. A more formal situation requires more attention to syntax and social conventions (for instance, "hello, pleased to meet you" rather than "hi there, honey!"). Students who do not understand the pragmatics aspects of language typically struggle as they attempt to interpret the sender's message.

•••••••••••••••

Just like oral language, written language involves a sender and a receiver.

•••••••••••••••

Authors also use a variety of styles to convey their message. Readers must be able to understand the author's purpose and point of view to comprehend effectively. The pragmatic aspects of reading also include the figurative language that authors may use to convey their messages. Students who are unable to ascertain the purpose of a written piece (as satire, comedy, fact-based, and so on), or who are unable to convey their purpose to the reader, will struggle with reading comprehension and written expression.

LITERACY AND CHILDREN WITH COMMUNICATIVE DISORDERS

The take-away message here is that SLPs already hold a great deal of knowledge related to facilitating strong literacy skills. We know that language and literacy are connected across many different parameters. We know that children who do not have a strong base in oral language will most likely have difficulty learning to read and write well. So, it is obviously of no surprise that a substantial number of the students on our caseloads are either already struggling readers or are at risk for reading delay or failure.

I do not advocate that SLPs replace reading teachers. However, I DO believe that it is appropriate and important for us to facilitate literacy however and whenever we can. This doesn't mean abandoning IEP goals or becoming nothing more than glorified tutors for our students. Rather, it means looking to the research to determine what skills are the most critical for students to develop in terms of learning to read and then finding ways to weave this into what we do in therapy—or in our collaborative work in classrooms, clinics, preschools, or with parents—to facilitate the development of BOTH oral and written language.

> Given the strong link between language and literacy, speech-language pathologists have increasingly taken the lead in designing and providing intervention programs that support development in both domains.

Introduction

PUT READING FIRST

Luckily for us, the question of what skills are the most critical for the development of literacy has already been addressed. In 2000, the National Reading Panel published the results of a comprehensive analysis of the research literature undertaken to identify instructional strategies that consistently led to reading success.

After examining data from thousands of empirical investigations, five skills were identified as being the most critical in developing strong literacy skills—in other words, "what works" in teaching children to read successfully. These five areas of concentration have been adapted by many schools and other educational entities as the foundation for building their reading programs. They are:

- ❖ **Phonemic awareness**
- ❖ **Phonics**
- ❖ **Reading fluency**
- ❖ **Vocabulary**
- ❖ **Text comprehension**

The first time I saw this list, I realized that SLPs have been addressing most of these skills in the oral mode for decades. Increasing phonemic awareness, building vocabulary knowledge, addressing oral fluency, and facilitating language comprehension has long been a part of traditional intervention for children with communicative disorders. In other words, most SLPs are already supporting literacy—we just didn't always know it, or know how to communicate what we were, and are, doing to facilitate written language to others.

Shifting our focus to the written mode just means expanding our efforts and thinking beyond oral language comprehension to the comprehension of the written word as well (text comprehension). Same concept—just perhaps tackled from a slightly different perspective.

It is important to understand that none of these five components is a complete program in and of itself. In fact, effective instruction includes attention to ALL FIVE components (plus one additional consideration that will come later in this book), delivered **systematically** and **intensively** at the appropriate level for each student.

Building Better Readers

HOW THIS BOOK WORKS

Once we embrace the idea that reading and writing is a subset of speaking and listening (think Language/Literacy Hierarchy) and, in fact, is just another mode of language, we can build activities that facilitate the development of literacy along with our more traditional oral language intervention strategies related to form, content, and use.

So, in the pages that follow, you will find a chapter devoted to each of the skills identified by the National Reading Panel—plus the final chapter which is devoted to nurturing a love of reading. Each chapter includes (in this order):

- An *introductory section* that includes a summary of research-supported information regarding the targeted skill area. The background information provided here, unless otherwise noted, comes from the studies that were part of the meta-analysis of the research related to literacy that is summarized in the National Reading Panel report.

- A variety of *strategies and activities*, including examples of appropriate children's literature, that support the development of that particular skill.

- A collection of *resources* such as book lists, activity sheets, websites, and/or other materials that support the development of that skill as well as the specific activities provided in the chapter.

The appendix provides on-line resources for Informal Reading Inventories, which are very useful for establishing baseline data for progress monitoring. A list of additional references and recommended readings are also provided here.

You may make copies of any of the resources marked as "reproducible for educational use" to use with your students or as a means of teaching other professionals or parents about language and literacy development. For ease of use, all reproducibles can also be downloaded from the Dynamic Resources website (www.dynamic-resource.org).

HAPPY READING!!

All reproducibles are available for free download at www.dynamic-resources.org

Introduction Resources

Primary Reference

National Institute of Child Health and Human Development. (2000). Report of the National Reading Panel. Teaching children to read: An evidence-based assessment of the scientific research literature on reading and its implications for reading instruction (NIH Publication No. 00-4769). Washington, DC: U.S. Government Printing Office.

Introduction Resources

THE LANGUAGE LITERACY HIERARCHY NARRATIVE

How to Use this Narrative

- ☐ Download the animated language-literacy hierarchy slide from www.dynamic-resources.org. (Click on Building Better Readers Tab then on Resources) *If you are unable to download the animated slide, email shari@dynamic-resources.org and I will send it to you!)*
- ☐ Read through the narrative, advancing or clicking each time you see the 🏷 symbol.
- ☐ Feel free to use your own words and/or improvise.
- ☐ Practice, practice, practice!

Script

The best way to demonstrate the importance of oral language to reading and writing, and ultimately all school subjects, is to demonstrate it using the Language/Literacy Hierarchy.

At the base of this pyramid is receptive oral language, LISTENING. This is the foundation of all learning, it is the first area to develop, and it is the largest area of development.

Think about how babies learn to talk. They can understand what you tell them long before they can say the words.

For instance, A 10-month old baby turns to look for Daddy when someone says "Daddy." Similarly, adults also have a much larger listening vocabulary (that is, words they can understand) than their speaking vocabulary.

For example, you could probably understand parts of a lecture on brain surgery, but you probably aren't ready to go and GIVE a lecture on the same topic!

Building Better Readers

The next level is expressive oral language, or TALKING. This area is slightly smaller than receptive language since you understand many more words than you actually use in your spoken vocabulary.

Obviously, you don't use words in oral communication that you don't understand (part of your receptive vocabulary)—Although there are people I know whom I suspect are doing this!

But for most of us, the size of our expressive language vocabulary is directly dependent on the size of our receptive vocabulary.

The same is true for children. A child who doesn't know what a giraffe is, won't use the word "giraffe" in conversation.

*The next level is receptive **written** language, or READING.*

*Now, you might be able to sound out a word like this....(Write on the board—or spell aloud—a word that is easy to decode, but not well known. My favorite is **gaskin**, but, depending on the audience, I have also used jaggar, aglet, and spasmophonia.)*

Can anyone read this word? (Select volunteer or choose someone).

Good! Now what does it mean? (Hopefully, your audience member will be able to decode the word, but be clueless regarding what it means.)

Then, would you say that you READ that word? I would agree that you DECODED it well - but if you don't know what the word means, how does that help you read and comprehend text?

What if a child had no idea what an owl is. Even if he or she could sound out the word, would that be reading? No, of course not. In order to truly read a word (not just sound out a bunch of letters) you must be able to comprehend its meaning.

So, your reading vocabulary is directly dependent on the size of your oral language base. (In case you were wondering, a gaskin is the upper thigh muscle on the hind leg of a horse. I'll let you figure out the others yourself).

*The fourth level, receptive **written** language or WRITING, is directly dependent*

on the size of your reading vocabulary.

In the same way as with oral language, you do not write words you cannot read. Consequently, your writing abilities are limited by your reading abilities.

On the very top are all the other academic areas that require oral and written skills in order to be proficient. These include math, social studies, English, science, and even physical education!

Now, as interesting as this all is, it is not the most impressive thing about this slide!

Let's say that a child enters school with a slightly smaller than average receptive vocabulary. This could be for any reason. Maybe he or she has not had a chance to visit a farm or a zoo or a grocery store. Maybe there is an underlying problem with language development. Maybe he or she was not read to or has a mild hearing loss.

Whatever the reason, this would mean that the child's **receptive** oral language base is going to be reduced.

That means that child's **expressive** oral language is also going to be somewhat smaller

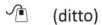 (ditto)

—which means his or her **reading** potential is also decreased.

This decreases the size of the **writing** base

Building Better Readers

—and when you see what has happened to the size of the top tier

—you no longer wonder why so many children are having trouble in math and science!

This is how the Language/Literacy Hierarchy will look when you are done. It's a powerful visual.

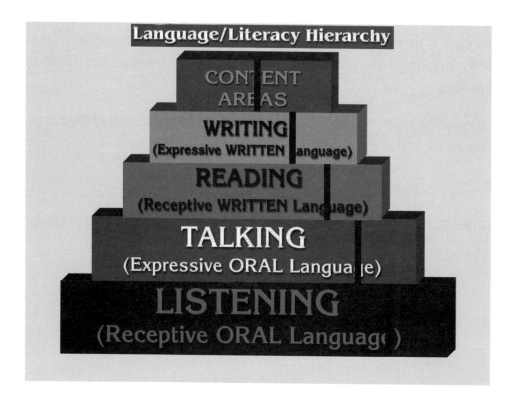

Introduction Resources

CHAPTER 2

Phonemic Awareness

Phonemic Awareness is the ability to hear and understand how the sounds of spoken language work together to make words. It is sometimes confused with the larger umbrella term of *phonological awareness*. However, while the latter involves learning to be aware of ANY size sound unit (e.g., words, syllables), phonemic awareness is the discrete, and more advanced, skill of being able identify and manipulate the individual sounds (phonemes) in words.

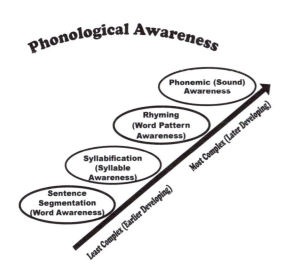

The figure here provides a quick visual review of the components of phonological awareness. Developmentally, children must first learn to identify larger units of sound (such as words) and progress toward smaller units (syllables and eventually phonemes). So, each of the skills related to phonological awareness is important to the development of literacy. (As a rule of thumb, the younger the child, the larger the unit of sound targeted).

However, given this, it is the discrete skill of phonemic awareness that the National Reading Panel found was most highly correlated with reading success.

Recall that phonemes are the smallest unit of *sound* in spoken language. They are not the same as letters (often referred to as graphemes) because letters are ***not*** sounds. So, although educators often talk about "silent letters," this is actually a misnomer. Letters only *represent* sounds—and in English, they don't do a very good job! For example, the sound /k/ can be represented by the letter *c* or *k* or even *ck* or *ch*. Vowels are even worse. Consider the word pairs *go* and *show*, *through* and *blue*, *bright* and *pie*. Each pair has the same vowel sound (phoneme), but is represented by a different letter or set of letters (graphemes).

The good news is that study results are impressive in terms of demonstrating that explicit, systematic instruction targeting phonemic awareness is highly effective:

> under a variety of teaching conditions

> with a variety of learners

> across a range of age and grade levels.

Of all the skills related to phonological awareness, the ability to hear and manipulate sounds—phonemic awareness—was the most highly correlated with reading success.

Building Better Readers

> **Sample Phonemic Awareness Tasks**
>
> • • • • • • • • • •
>
> **Isolation**
> *What sound does cookie start with?*
>
> **Identity**
> *What sound begins me, might, and many?*
>
> **Blending**
> *What word is /b/ /l/ /g/?*
>
> **Segmentation**
> *How many sounds in dark?*
>
> **Substitution**
> *The word is "hat." What word do you get when you change the /t/ to /m/?*

Tasks typically associated with proficiency in phonemic awareness, as summarized in the sidebar, include phoneme isolation, phoneme identity, sound segmentation and blending, and phoneme substitution. Each contributes to creating critical levels of competency related to the sounds of language.

Not surprisingly, children who can hear and isolate the sounds of a language are likely to have an easier time establishing the sound/symbol relationships necessary to learn to read and spell than children who are lacking proficiency in this skill. Students can do a better job navigating the twists and turns of English phonics when they have the prerequisite phonemic awareness skills in place.

Also of no great surprise, children with speech or/language deficits are at risk for delayed development of phonemic awareness—most likely for the very same reasons they have difficulty extracting information from the spoken environment for language processing. Consequently, targeting phonemic awareness is an appropriate and empirically-supported strategy for facilitating literacy skills for a majority of children on speech/language caseloads.

Phonemic awareness activities can be introduced in the preschool years and are appropriate through age 8 and beyond. Study results indicate that working on only a few of these tasks at a time is more effective than working on all of them, so it is important to target tasks that are appropriate for each child's skill level. Further, activities related to both phonological or phonemic awareness are implemented without trying to make any connections to letters of the alphabet. We are not trying to establish sound-symbol relationships, but we are laying the groundwork for building toward that skill.

As mentioned previously, young children progress from an awareness of larger units of speech sounds to smaller units. Consequently, for preschoolers, it is appropriate to begin by encouraging an awareness of syllables and rhyming (phonological awareness skills) as a precursor to targeting phonemic awareness. We want to give preschoolers multiple opportunities to play with sounds and the sound patterns that make up language prior to asking them to work with individual sound units (phonemes). For instance, you can count words or syllables by clapping, tapping, or marching to encourage the basic idea that the stream of speech can be broken down into smaller chunks. Fingerplays and stories with strong rhyming sequences can also contribute to the development of phonological—and, eventually—phonemic awareness.

Consequently, only after children have established word and syllable awareness is it appropriate to move on to phonemic awareness activities—regardless of age! In other words, you may find you need to "back up" and work on more global phonological awareness activities with older children who have not developed these skills or you can move forward to activities that are aimed at facilitating phonemic awareness with preschoolers who are ready for that.

Replicated across numerous studies is the finding that improvement in phonemic awareness correlates strongly with improvements in reading and spelling. Consequently, it is never too late to work on phonemic awareness. I am going to say that again with emphasis added: **IT IS NEVER TOO LATE TO WORK ON PHONEMIC AWARENESS.** I have been dismayed to find that in some school districts, phonemic awareness instruction is discontinued at a specific and predetermined age or grade regardless of whether or not the student has mastered this critical skill. However, abandoning phonemic awareness instruction just because a child has reached a certain age is like trying to build a skyscraper without the proper foundation. You may make some progress, but eventually there will be a spectacular crash. Advocating for continued instruction in phonemic awareness until mastery is a critical task for anyone responsible for the education of our children.

SLPs are actually masters of phonemic awareness instruction. It is a common part of intervention to improve articulation. Think of how many times we ask a child to isolate his or her "sound" in a word! "Miranda, is your sound in that word?" or "Zach, can you use a word with your sound at the beginning?" Further, SLPs understand the difference between phonemic awareness and phonics. So, when asking what sound begins "moo, milk, and mice," we teach children /m/ rather than "em." In other words, we've been doing (virtually forever) what the current literature base tells us is a critical skill for building better readers.

Whether you are in the classroom or the therapy room, incorporating phonemic awareness activities into your routine takes only minutes a day and can pay big dividends for your students in terms of facilitating their literacy skills.

> *Abandoning phonemic awareness instruction just because a child has reached a certain age is like trying to build a skyscraper without the proper foundation.*

STRATEGIES FOR BUILDING
PHONEMIC AWARENESS

Phonemic Awareness

BOOKS! BOOKS! BOOKS!

An effective and natural way to provide children with opportunities to play with sounds is through the use of appropriate children's literature. In fact, I incorporate books into therapy as often and as much as I can. Beyond the targeted skill, books naturally help facilitate vocabulary development, provide models for reading fluency, promote lots of opportunities for oral language interactions, and create an awareness for children that books can be fun! (You'll find a recurring theme for me is, "A nose in a book is a good thing!") Here are some of my favorites: (You can find more in the *Resources* section of this chapter.)

Books That Encourage an Awareness of Sounds and Sound Patterns

There's a Wocket in My Pocket (Dr. Seuss)

Dr. Seuss is a master at engaging children in rhyme by mixing nonsense words with "real" words. In this story a child creates rhymes about everyday objects around his house such as, "there's a jamp in my lamp" and "a yottle in my bottle." Obviously, we can extend this by having children create their own rhymes about what in THEIR house, or classroom or backyard or playground or……wherever!

Bendomelina /The Cat Who Wore a Pot on Her Head (Jan Slepian)

Bendomelina, a cat from a large family, doesn't like all the noise in her house. So, she puts a pot on her head – which happens to cover her ears— to get some peace and quiet. Unfortunately, this makes it difficult for her to understand what people are saying to her. When her mother must go help a sick friend, she takes Bendomelina with her to run errands. All kinds of chaos ensues as Bendomelina mixes up her mother's instructions. For instance, when her mother tells her to "put the soup on the heat," she decides she must have said, "Iron the meat"—and she does! The cat family also ends up with "soap in the cake" (instead of "fish on to bake") and chairs hung on the wall (instead of "sweep out the hall").

Building Better Readers

Down by the Bay (Raffi)

This book is particularly fun because it is actually one of Raffi's songs written down and illustrated with child-friendly pictures. The natural echoing pattern (adult reads/sings, child reads/sings the same line) encourages active participation and vocabulary development as well as phonological awareness and reading fluency. As with the previous book, we can encourage children to create their own rhymes once they have learned the basic pattern (e.g.," Did you ever see a cat wearing a hat—down by the bay.")

Ook the Book and Other Silly Rhymes (Lissa Rovetch)

In addition to "Ook" the Book, the characters in this book include "Ug" the Bug, "Ing" the Thing, and "Eep" the Sheep. Each is introduced using a fun rhyme that is loaded with opportunities to play with, and contrast, sounds. Here's an example:

I am Ow. Ow the cow.

I can bark. Bow wow wow.

Don't ask me why, don't ask me how.

I am just that kind of cow!

Or this one:

I am At.

At the cat.

Do you see Pat?

He is my rat.

I sat on Pat so he is flat.

This is a zany romp with colorful engaging pictures that literally begs children to read along and join the sound play. A must for your collection!

Phonemic Awareness

Cocka Doodle Moo (Bernard Most)

In this story, the rooster awakens one morning to a sore throat and can't say "Cock-a-Doodle-Do." This means he cannot wake up the sleeping farmer. If the farmer doesn't wake up, nothing will get done around the farm. This is a big problem! The cow thinks she can help and so she tries to say "Cock-a-Doodle-Do." Unfortunately, the best she can do is "Mock-a-Moodle-Moo." It doesn't wake up the farmer. She tries again: "Sock-A-Moodle-Do?" "Clock-A-Noodle-Poo?" The books continues in this manner—playing with all manner of sounds in the beginning position of the rooster's crow. Great fun to read and role play!

The Hungry Thing (Jan Slepien)

One day, the Hungry Thing arrives in a town with a sign around his neck that says "Feed Me!" Each time he points to his sign, he says a nonsense word that just happens to rhyme with a word that is, in fact, food. The townspeople all try to figure out what he wants to eat. However, the only one smart enough to decipher what the Hungry Things is actually asking for is one little boy (with a good ear for rhyme!). The townspeople eventually catch on and when the Hungry Thing asks for "tickles", he gets pickles. "Shmancakes" is pancakes and "thread" is, of course, bread.

This book provides lots of opportunities for active engagement as children join in with the characters from this silly town to try to guess what the Hungry Things wants to eat.

Books That Highlight Alliteration and/or Specific Phonemes

SLPs target phonemic awareness every time we ask students to listen for "their" sound. Books that are rich in alliteration (a string of words that all begin with the same sound) or include multiple instances of a specific phoneme help make sounds more salient to the listener—fostering phonemic awareness. Pairing books such as these with articulation and phonology intervention is a great way to target both literacy and IEP goals.   Here's a few to get you started.

Some Smug Slug (Pamela Duncan Edwards)

A very smug slug "senses a slope" and "saunters" on up. His friends, among them a spider, a sparrow, and a skink, try to stop his ascent but the slug is unfazed and continues on his way. This book is chock full of great vocabulary as well as numerous words that start with /s/ (although some are actually "sh," but we can work that into the lesson). Caution: this book does not have a traditional happy ending. (That smug slug ends up as a succulent snack for a sly toad). There are other "s" creatures depicted throughout the book and it's fun to find the "S" shapes hidden in each picture.

Building Better Readers

Faint Frogs Feeling Feverish (Lillian Obligato)

Silly animals caper across the pages of this book described by zany alliterative phrases ranging from "Auk arresting ape" to "Zebra zipping zipper." It also builds vocabulary and critical thinking skills.

Do be aware that the vowel alliterations used in this book—and most others that try to use alliteration with vowels—pairs multiple sounds with a specific grapheme. In English, we only have five letters to represent more than 20 vowel sounds, so it's a bit hard to manage vowel alliterations. (For instance, "auk arresting ape" actually starts with three different sounds: /ɔ/, /ə/, and /eɪ/.)

The Word Menders Series (Dynamic Resources)

This book series was written **by** SLPs **for** SLPs. Each story is built around minimal pairs that target a specific phonological process. Books are written using the principles established by the National Reading Panel so children are also provided with opportunities to engage in the story, to predict rhyming words, and to chime in on repetitive phrases throughout the story. Each book also includes a set of flashcards of the minimal pairs from the story that store in a handy pocket in the back cover of the book.

Pants on Ants: Initial Consonant Deletion

Go By Goat: Final Consonant Deletion

The Bark Park: Voicing Contrasts

My Cow Can Bow: Front/Back Contrasts

Sail By a Tail: Stopping

The Sound System Series (coming soon ~ Dynamic Resources)

This series is currently being developed by Margot Kelman with Barbara Hodson that will feature stories that target specific phonemes. This is sure to be an outstanding resource, so watch for it!

> **A comprehensive list of books that highlight specific phonemes can be found in the *Phonemic Awareness Resources* section of this chapter.**

Phonemic Awareness

SONGS! SONGS! SONGS!

Songs, fingerplays, and nursery rhymes, long a staple of preschool classrooms, provide multiple benefits to young children in areas such as phonological awareness, vocabulary development, and pragmatics. Most preschool teachers instinctively use songs such as Willowby, Wallowby, Woo (the Elephant Song) or the Name Game song ("Hanna, Fanna, Fo, Fanna") to help children learn to rhyme —and this is good practice.

Phonemic awareness can also be facilitated by modifying well-known songs and rhymes to emphasize specific phonemes. All it takes is a little imagination. Here's a few to get you started!

Old MacDonald Had a Farm

Sing the song as you normally would, but when you get to the chorus, add a sound at the beginning of the chorus syllables that matches the initial sound of name of the animal.

Like This

Old McDonald had a farm

Ee-i-ee-i-oh!

*....and on that farm he had a **D**og*

***D**ee-**D**i-**D**ee-**D**i-**D**oh!*

*....and on that farm he had a **C**ow*

***K**ee-**K**i-**K**ee-**K**i-**K**oh!*

*.....and on that farm he had a **H**orse*

***H**ee-**H**i-**H**ee-**H**i-**H**oh!*

*...and on that farm he had a **G**oose*

***G**ee-**G**i-**G**ee-**G**i-**G**oh!*

Building Better Readers

The Farmer in the Dell

Sing the song as usual, but match the first sound of who or what was "taken" to the first sound in the chorus.

Like This

*The **f**armer in the dell, the **f**armer in the dell,*

***F**i-**F**o the **F**erio, the **f**armer in the dell*

*The farmer takes a **w**ife, the farmer takes a **w**ife*

***W**i-**W**o the **W**erio, the farmer takes a **w**ife*

*The wife takes a **ch**ild, the wife takes a **ch**ild*

***Ch**i-**Ch**o the **Ch**erio the wife takes a **ch**ild*

*The child takes a **d**og, the child takes a **d**og*

***D**i-**D**o the **D**erio, the child takes a **d**og*

Don't be constrained by the actual words of the song. It's also fun to think of new "things" that end up in the dell that aren't in the original song.

*The farmer takes a **z**ebra, the farmer takes a **z**ebra*

***Z**i-**Z**o the **Z**erio, the farmer takes a **z**ebra*

*The zebra takes a **l**ion, the zebra takes a **l**ion*

***L**i-**L**o the **L**erio, the zebra takes a **l**ion*

Phonemic Awareness

The Sound Song

Sing this to the tune of the chorus of *I've Been Working on the Railroad*. Be sure to say the SOUND not the letter at the beginning of each new verse.

/f/ is a sound I know!
/f/ is a sound I know-oh-oh-oh
/f/ is a sound I know
/f/ is a sound I know
Fee-fi- fiddlee-i-foh
Fee-fi-fiddlee-i-foh-foh-foh-foh
Fee-fi-fiddlee-i-foh
/f/ is a sound I know!

/t/ is a sound I know
/t/ is a sound I know-oh-oh-oh
/t/ is a sound I know
/t/ is a sound I know!
Tee-ti-tiddlee-i-toh
Tee-ti-tiddlee-i-toh-toh-toh-toh
Tee-ti-tiddlee-i-toh
/t/ is a sound I know!

/b/ is a sound I know
/b/ is a sound I know-oh-oh-oh
/b/ is a sound I know
/b/ is a sound I know!
Bee-bi-biddlee-i-boh
Bee-bi-biddlee-i-boh-boh-boh-boh
Bee-bi-biddlee-i-boh
/b/ is a sound I know!

You can make this song even more challenging (and more fun) by introducing consonant clusters...

/sk/ is a sound I know
/sk/ is a sound I know-oh-oh-oh
/sk/ is a sound I know
/sk/ is a sound I know!
Skee-ski-skiddlee-i-skoh
Skee-ski-skiddlee-i-skoh-skoh-skoh-skoh
Skee-ski-skiddlee-i-skoh
/sk/ is a sound I know!

Building Better Readers

ACTIVITIES FOR PHONEME IDENTITY, ISOLATION, AND SEGMENTATION

This set of activities target phoneme identify, isolation, and/or segmentation. The focus is on helping children hear, manipulate, and identify individual sounds.

HEAD OR TOE?

This activity helps children isolate sounds and identify their position in a word. Start by highlighting the sound you want them to listen for in isolation. Then, say a word that has the sound either at the beginning or at the end. If the sound starts the word, the children touch their heads. At the end, they touch their toes!

Example

Today we are going to listen for the /m/ sound. Everyone say /m/, /m/, /m/. (Feel free to name this the "yummy" sound or some other label if you wish.)

Now, listen closely. I'm going to say a word and your job is to listen for the /m/ sound. If you hear the sound at the beginning of the word, put your hands on your head. Like this! **M**onkey. *I hear /m/ at the beginning so everyone put their hands on their head!*

Now, how about "ham?" I hear the /m/ at the end of the word, so everyone touch their toes! Remember, beginning, hands on your head – end, touch your toes.

Let's try it!

Meat   *(Child/ren put hands on head)*

Dru**m**   *(Child/ren touch toes)*

Extension/Variation

❖ Eventually, you can add the middle sound – such as ha**mm**er. Children would then put their hands on their hips.

Phonemic Awareness

PACK IT UP

Explain to students that the class (or group) is going to pretend we are going on a trip. We need to help our friends find things to put in their suitcase that begin with the same sound as their name. Choose a student and say their name, emphasizing the first sound. As appropriate, you can isolate the sound for the class to be sure everyone hears it.

Example

❏   **Adult:** *Our friend* **Brianna** *needs to fill up her suitcase. What sound do we hear at the beginning of Brianna's name? That's right we hear /b/! So, what can we put in her suitcase?*

Child/ren: **B**rushes! **B**ananas! **B**eans! *****B**icycle! **B**arbie dolls! *****B**rother! *****B**aseballs!

Adult: *How about a kite? (Everyone shouts) NO!!!*

❏   **Adult:** *Our friend* **Drew** *needs to fill up his suitcase. What sound do we hear at the beginning of Drew's name? That's right! We hear /d/!*

Children: *****D**ucks! **D**iamonds! **D**oughnuts! **D**rums! *****D**illy Bars! **D**aisies! *****D**inosaurs! **D**ust Fluffies!

✱   It's fun to think of silly things that we KNOW won't fit or wouldn't be good to put in a suitcase (which is the seed of an entirely different game about silly and real).

THROW IT OUT THE WINDOW!

Explain that you have three things (or more as student/s get better at this task) in your house, but one of them doesn't belong. The child/ren's job is to listen carefully to the first sound in the words and pick the one that doesn't belong. Then we will "throw it out the window!"

Example

Adult: I have shoes, sheep, and a horse in my house. Which one should we throw out the window?

Child/ren: The horse!!!

Adult: You're right! The horse doesn't belong. It starts with /h/. Shoes and sheep start with /ʃ/. What are we going to do with it?

Everyone: Throw it out the window! (All laugh hysterically.)

You can also do this with a final sound. Be sure to remind the child/ren to listen to the LAST sound of the word (this is a *much* harder task).

Adult: I have a ham, a drum, and a bug in my house. Which one doesn't belong?

Child/ren: The ham?

Adult: Not quite! I want to keep that ham. It ends with the same sound as the drum. Both of them end with /m/. But the bug ends with a different sound. It ends with /g/. So what should we do with that bug?

All: Throw it out the window!!

I recently heard from some Building Better Readers workshop participants who reported that they created a cardboard window and employed pictures and props that could actually be "thrown out the window!

• •

Students demonstrated positive outcomes related to phonemic awareness and everyone thoroughly enjoyed the activity.

Phonemic Awareness

Activities for Sounding Segmentation and Sound Blending

Sound segmentation, or separating out each individual sound in a spoken word, has been described as one of the more difficult skills for children to acquire. To develop this skill, we want to provide activities that help children hear the individual phonemes. **Sound blending**, on the other hand, is one of the easier skills to acquire. This is not surprising since sound blending is the reverse process of sound segmentation. Consequently, once segmentation has been mastered, blending is a relatively easy task.

This next set of activities target sound segmentation and blending—some target both!

HAPPY HANDS

This activity is easy to do with a group of children and works with all ages!

Method

- ❑ Student/s start with their hands pressed together in front of their bodies.
- ❑ Adult says a word.
- ❑ Children say each sound in the word while simultaneously moving their hands apart—each time a little farther for each sound.
- ❑ Then have them close their hands again while saying the "whole" word.

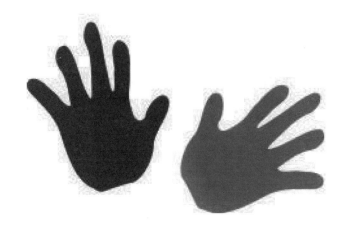

HEAD, SHOULDERS, KNEES, AND TOES

Provide a word that is made up of one to four phonemes. Students segment by saying each sound in the word while touching their head, shoulders, knees, and toes as appropriate. Always end by having the child/children say the word.

Examples

Word: "me"

Students say: /m/ (touch head) /i/ touch shoulders

Word: "pig"

Students say: /p/ (touch head), /ɪ/(touch shoulders), /g/ (touch toes). "Pig."

Word: " I"

Students say: /aɪ/ (touch head only) "I."

Word: "penny"

Students say: /p/ (touch head), /ɛ/ (touch shoulders), /n/ (touch knees), /ɪ/ (touch toes) "Penny."

> **Find books, websites, and patterns to facilitate phonemic awareness in the *Phonemic Awareness Resources* section of this chapter**

Phonemic Awareness

SOUND TRAIN

Another way to help students segment sounds is to use a sound train. This requires some prep time in that you need to create a train (or take advantage of the Sound Train provided in the *Resources* section of this chapter and at www.dynamic-resources.org). The child/ren (or modeling adult) moves a finger from the engine toward the caboose as a word is said aloud, touching one train car for each sound. This helps reinforce that words have a beginning (the engine) and an end (nearer the caboose)—just like a train!

A *Sound Train Worksheet* is available in the **Phonemic Awareness Resources** section of this chapter.

Building Better Readers

PICTURE PIECES

This activity provides hands-on, concrete practice with sound segmentation as students can physically pull a word apart sound-by-sound and then reassemble it back into the original word. You can have students bring in pictures or create your own from software or internet images.

Method

- ❏ Laminate pictures and cut into pieces that represent the number of sounds in the word.
- ❏ Assemble the picture and then have the child say each sound while sliding the pieces apart.
- ❏ Reverse the activity by having the child assemble the picture while sliding the pieces together.
- ❏ Once together, be sure to have the child say the whole word.
- ❏ See the example on the next page for a visual representation of how this activity works.

Extension/Variations

- ❖ You can make this even more fun by mixing up pieces from several pictures and having the child search for pieces to complete a picture before doing the activity.

- ❖ The first word I often choose to use for this activity is the student's name. Take a picture of the student and print it out. Cut into pieces to match the number of phonemes in the child's name. Once they can consistently segment and reassemble the sounds of their name, tape the picture together permanently and hang on the wall. You will soon have a phonemic awareness wall of fame!

> You can find more pictures to use for this activity in the *Resources* section of this chapter and at www.dynamic-resources.org.

Phonemic Awareness

/p/

/ɪ/

/g/

"pig"

Building Better Readers

BOX IT UP

A well-known, well-researched, and effective strategy to facilitate sound segmentation is the use of Elkonin boxes. This activity gets its name from Russia psychologist D.B. Elkonin who was instrumental in developing this technique to facilitate early reading skills. Similar to *Picture Pieces*, the idea is to help children visualize each sound as an individual entity through the use of physical manipulation. The basic procedure is fairly simple.

Method

- ❏ Provide each student with a template made up of a series boxes (you may choose to laminate them) and a number of tokens such as chippers, small blocks, or even kernels of corn.

- ❏ As you say a word aloud, students move the tokens into a box—one token/box for each sound.

- ❏ Be SURE to say the word aloud so the focus remains on listening to sounds rather than decoding.

- ❏ Have students say each sound they hear aloud as they move their tokens into the boxes—and then again when they take them out.

- ❏ See the facing page for examples.

Extension/Variations

- ❖ Battery Operated "click" lights are a great alternative to Elkonin boxes. Line them up and have students click one for each sound. Too cool!

- ❖ Another fun, inexpensive alternative is to use paint sample strips from your local hardware as your Elkonin boxes. Students can choose their favorite color combinations and it's zero prep work for you!

- ❖ Clip colorful clothespins on the side of a box or any other handy surface. One for each sound. You can increase the skill level by using different color clips to represent initial, medial, and final sounds or any other code that meets student needs.

Paint strip samples make fabulous, colorful (and free!) Elkonin boxes.

44

Robertson

Phonemic Awareness

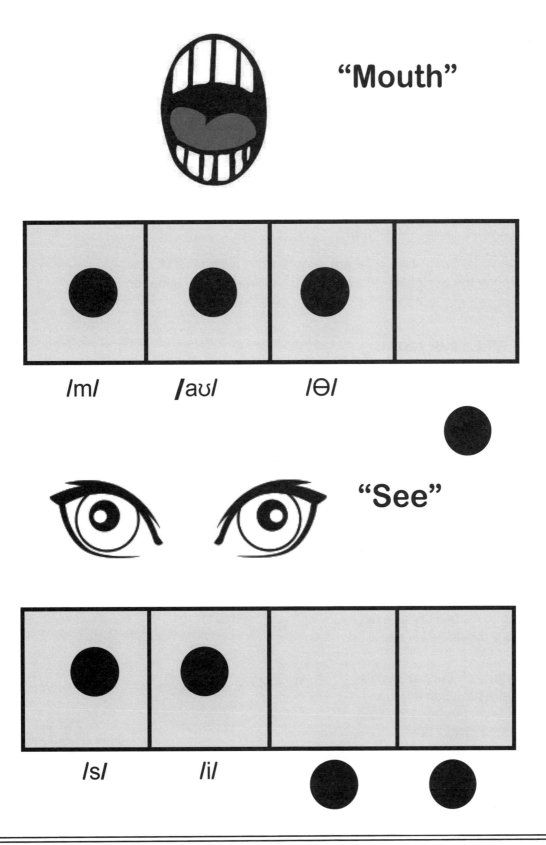

Building Better Readers

JUMP, FROG, JUMP!

Here's another activity for segmenting sounds that uses a principle similar to Elkonin boxes. It changes things up in that it uses the children's entire bodies rather than just fingers or chips. You can also use this activity to segment syllables for younger children.

Method

- ❑ Place four mats or carpet squares on the floor (hula hoops also work!).
- ❑ Say a word aloud (1-4 sounds).
- ❑ Have your "frogs" (aka children) jump from "lily pad" to "lily pad"—one for each sound in the word (okay, they are mats, but we have imaginations).

MAKE SURE YOUR FROGS "CROAK" EACH SOUND AS THEY JUMP FROM MAT TO MAT!

Extension/Variations

❖ Give each child a laminated page with four or five lily pads on it.

❖ Students use their finger to jump from lily pad to lily pad saying each sound as they touch the lily pad.

❖ A froggy finger puppet makes this even more fun! (See *Resources Section* of this chapter for a full-size version of this activity sheet.)

I KNOW SOMETHING/SOMEONE

This is a simple, but effective, way to help children learn about blending sounds to make a word. It takes almost no prep which is always good for busy clinicians and teachers. It's best to use this at a quiet time when you have students' attention.

Examples

Adult: *I know (or see) something that starts with /b/ and ends with /ʊk/ (b-ook). What is it?*

Student/s: *Book!*

Adult: *I know someone whose name starts with /p/ and ends with /it/ (P-ete). Who is it?*

Student/s: *Pete!*

You can also partition the sounds this way

Adult: *I see something that starts with /koʊ/ and ends with /t/ (coa-t). What is it?*

Student/s: *Coat!*

If this is too hard, try syllables

Adult: *I know someone whose name starts with /ti/ and ends with /nə/. (Ti-na). Who is it?*

Student/s: *Tina!*

Once students get the hang of the activity, it's time to have them create the riddle questions. This increases the difficulty factor slightly and facilitates both sound segmentation and sound blending.

Building Better Readers

The *I Know Something* game is an excellent lead-in activity for introducing the concept of sound deletion.

> ### Sound Deletion
> •
>
> Deletion of sounds is a higher level skill that requires children to manipulate the sounds while holding the word in memory. Many researchers suggest that sound deletion tasks are not appropriate for children under the age of 7 (cognitively) and that children should have a grasp of phoneme segmentation prior to introducing phoneme deletion.

Example:

Adult: I'm thinking of something that starts with /m/ and ends with /ɪt/ (m-eat). What is it?

Student/s: Meat!

Adult: Now say meat without the /m/. What is it?

Student/s: Eat!

Here are some examples that are a little harder:

Adult: I'm thinking of something that starts with /l/ and ends with /aɪt/. What is it?

Student/s: Light!

Adult: Now, say light without the /t/. What is it?

Student/s: Lie!

Adult: I'm thinking of something that starts with /b/ and ends with /reɪn/. What is it?

Student/s: Brain!

Adult: Now, say brain without the /b/.

Student/s: Rain!

Phonemic Awareness

BLOCK ACTIVITIES

Block activities help children visualize the sound patterns of words using tangible manipulatives. You will need to provide each child with a set of blocks of various colors. For the most challenging activities, you will need four blocks each of 4 or 5 colors. For the less challenging tasks, you can use fewer blocks and colors.

Blocks of any size can be used—as long as they can be easily manipulated by the child/ren. I have used small one-inch blocks as well as larger wooden blocks. If you don't have blocks, you can really use any small manipulative such as magnetic "chippers," crayons, or even colored squares of heavy paper stock or cardboard. However, for the sake of this discussion, the term "blocks" will be used.

The tasks summarized in the tables on the following pages are presented in a general progression from easiest to most difficult. Use demonstrations and models liberally until the child/ren get the "hang" of the task. You will be surprised how fast most children pick this up (even those who have some learning challenges) and how much most children enjoy the activities.

Method

In a nutshell, sounds are represented by blocks—color doesn't matter except that children will learn to use the colors to differentiate one sound from another. So, for example, in the first task, children are asked to identify if two sounds are the same or different. Two sounds that are the same will be represented by two blocks of the same (any) color. Sounds that are not alike will be represented by two blocks of differing colors (again, the color doesn't matter—just that they are different).

Concentrate on one task at a time. Don't move on until the child is completing the task with a high level of accuracy (i.e., above 90%). Then, introduce the next task, but come back often to "visit" the easier tasks whenever you sense frustration. Keep the sessions short and provide lots of positive reinforcement! Feel free to experiment with your own tasks—or turn the tables and have the child be the "teacher" and you manipulate the blocks. Although I have never used it, a peer reviewer of this manual suggested that Lindamood offers a phonological awareness program that includes these types of block activities should you wish additional information in this area.

Building Better Readers

Prompt	Correct Response	Example Blocks (R=red, Y=yellow, B=blue)
Adult provides sounds: slight pause in between. /t/..../t/ /t/..../d/	Child lines up: Two blocks—same color Two blocks—different colors	R R R Y
Adult provides a series of sounds: slight pause in between /t/..../t/..../t/ /n/ /l/.../n/.../v/ /s/.../k/..../s/	Child lines up: Three blocks—same color One block—any color Three blocks—different colors Three blocks—first and last same color	R R R B B Y R Y B Y
Adult assigns a rime (vowel plus consonant) to a single block on the table. Adult touches this block and says: *This block says "ay." Now, show me "day."* *This block says "ow." Now show me "out."*	Child lays a different color block in front of the block designated as "ay." (Two blocks—one to represent "ay" and one to represent "d.") Child lays a different color block after the block designated as "ow." (Two blocks—one to represent "ow" and one to represent "t.")	"d" "ay" R Y ← Adult designates "ow" "t" B R ← Adult designates

Phonemic Awareness

Prompt	Correct Response	Example Blocks (R=red, Y=yellow, B=blue,
Adult cues by touching each block while saying the word: *This is "n..........ice."* *Now, show me "ice."* *This is "s........eed."* *Now show me "see."*	Child removes first block. Child removes second block.	"n" "ice" [R] [Y] [Y] "see" "d" [B] [R] [B]
Adult cues: *Show me "moo."* *Now, show me "zoo."* *Now, show me "up."* *Now, show me "us."*	Child lays down two blocks of different colors—one for "m" and second for "oo" of a different color. Child changes the first block to a different color. Child lays down two blocks of different colors—one for "uh" and one for "p" of a different color. Child changes the second block to a different color.	"m" "oo" [R] [Y] "z" "oo" [B] [Y] "uh" "p" [R] [B] "uh" "s" [B] [Y]
Adult cues by touching each sound while saying the word: *This is "b-ea-n"* *Now, show me "bee"*	Child removes final block.	"b" "ee" "n" [R] [B] [Y] [R] [B]

Building Better Readers

LINKING PHONEMIC AWARENESS AND SPELLING

Apel, Masterson, and Wilson-Fowler (2011) emphasize the importance of linking phonemic awareness to spelling. Since there is no such thing as silent **sound** (my emphasis), students need to understand that there must be **at least** one letter to represent each sound they hear in a word.

For example, a student hears three sounds in the word "*shout.*" Consequently, the student must be sure that there are at least three letters in the word when he/she spells it.

Of course, there can be more than one letter for each sound, as is true of "*shout*"; however, the critical concept is the there can be no **LESS** than one letter per sound/phoneme. Once this has been established, SLPs can work with students to help them activate knowledge of what they already know, and what they still may need to learn, about spelling a particular word.

SOUND STRINGS

To assist students in making this connection, Wasowicz, Apel, Masterson, & Whitney (2012) advocate the use of a Sound String. In this activity, students move a bead from one end of a string to another – one for each sound they hear. The authors suggest that this is a particularly appropriate method of phoneme segmentation for older students because the string can be held between the hands so that only the SLP/educator can see each student's answer.

Method

- ❑ Targeted word is said aloud with a designation of its role in language (e.g., noun, verb, adjective) and used in a sentence.

- ❑ Student moves a bead from one side of the string to the other for each sound they hear.

- ❑ Student then "plops" (quoting Kenn Apel from a recent workshop!) the sound string down at the top of his or her paper and writes at least one letter under each bead to represent each sound.

- ❑ SLP/educator then discusses the outcome including "other knowledge demonstrated by the student" regarding how they spelled the word.

Phonemic Awareness

Example

❏ **Adult:** *The word is **treats**: A plural noun. "Ice cream is one of my favorite treats."*

❏ **Student** *slides one bead for each sound heard. Then "plops" the sound string at the top of his or her paper and writes at least one letter for every bead. (Note that I created this sound string using eight beads threaded on a pipe cleaner).*

❏ **Adult:** *First **(and very importantly)** indicates that the student has the correct number of sounds and has written at least one letter for every sound. Then, provides additional feedback related to the student's spelling of the word. Here, we would identify the letters that are correct and also discuss that the vowel sound in this word is represented by two letters.*

> The use of Sounds Strings to facilitate spelling proficiency is fully described in ***SPELL-Links to Reading and Writing: A Word-Study Curriculum.***
> Find it at **www.learningbydesign.com**
> I highly recommend this powerful, evidence-driven spelling curriculum!

PUNCH IT UP!

I have successfully used a similar strategy for sound segmentation using a paper punch and post-it notes. Rather than moving beads, students punch one hole for each sound they hear. This highly-motivating activity can easily be adapted to include the "one sound = at least one letter" principle advocated by the authors of the SPELL-Links curriculum.

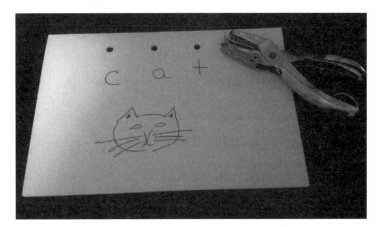

PHONEMIC AWARENESS RESOURCES

Phonemic Awareness Resources

BOOKS THAT FACILITATE PHONEMIC AWARENESS

Sound Play and Sound Manipulation	
The Bus for Us	Suzanne Bloom
An Ear is to Hear	Jan Slepian
Ape in a Cape	Fritz Eichenberg
Bendomelina (The Cat Who Wore a Pot on Her Head)	Jan Slepian
Cock-A-Doodle-Moo	Bernard Most
Down by the Bay	Raffi
Drat that Fat Cat	Pat Thompson
Hop on Pop	Dr. Seuss
I Heard Said the Bird	Polly Berrien Berends
Jake Bakes Cakes	Gerald Hawksley
Fabulous Fingerplays	Jane Kitson
Fox in Socks	Dr. Seuss
The Hungry Thing	Jan Slepian
Mice Are Nice	Judy Nayer
Ook the Book and Other Silly Rhymes	Lissa Rovetch
Pig In a Wig	Judy Nayer
Miss Bindergarten Gets Ready for Kindergarten	Joseph Slate
Mrs. McNosh Hangs Up Her Wash	Sarah Weeks
The Story of Mable at the Table with a Ladle	Lavelle Carlson
Rhyming Dust Bunnies	Jan Thomas
Runny Babbit: A Billy Sook (best for older students)	Shel Silverstein
There's a Wocket in my Pocket	Dr. Seuss

Building Better Readers

ALL SOUNDS	
The Sound System Series*	Margot Kelman with Barbara Hodson
/b/ and blends	
Bats at the Ballgame	Brian Lies
Boo Bunny	Kathryn Galbraith
Boo to a Goose	Mem Fox
Bubble Bear	Maxwell Higgins
It's Not Easy Being a Bunny	Marilyn Sadler
King Bidgood's in the Bathtub	Audrey Wood
/d/	
Detective Dog and the Disappearing Donuts	Valerie Garfield
Dinorella	Pamela Duncan Edwards
Duck on a Bike	David Shannon
Duck in a Truck	Jez Alborough
Hot Dog	Molly Coxe
/f/ and blends	
F is for Flag	Wendy Cheyette Lewison
Faint Frogs Feeling Feverish	Lillian Obligato
Fat Frogs on a Skinny Log	Sara Riches
Flashing Fire Engines	Tony Mitton
Follow Those Footprints	Christine Ricci
Four Famished Foxes and Fosdick	Pamela Duncan Edwards
Four Fur Feet	Margaret Wise Brown
The Great Fuzz Frenzy	Susan Stevens Crummel

Phonemic Awareness Resources

Ten Red Apples	Pat Hutchins
/g/ and blends	
Giggle, Giggle, Quack	Doreen Cronin
A Girl, a Goose, a Goat, and the Storm	David McPhail
Go Away, Big Green Monster	Ed Emberly
Goodnight Gorilla	Peggy Rathman
Goose on the Loose	Phil Roxbee Cox
Gorilla Be Good!	Maria Fleming
Gus	Modern Curriculum Press
One Guinea Pig is Enough	Kate Duke
Silly Little Goose	Nancy Tafuri
Ten Timid Ghosts	Jennifer O'Connell
Ten Timid Ghosts at Christmas	Jennifer O'Connell
There's a Billy Goat in the Garden	Laurel Dee Gugler
/k/ and blends	
The Cake that Mack Ate	Rose Robart
Capering Cows*	Shari Robertson
Clumsy Crab	Ruth Galloway
Cold Little Duck, Duck, Duck	Lisa Westberg Peters
There's a Cow in the Cabbage Patch	Clare Beaton
Click, Clack, Moo: Cows that Type	Doreen Cronin
The Clumsy Cowboy	Jane Bethell
Copycats	Maria Fleming
Eek!	Jez Alborough

Building Better Readers

From Head to Toe	Eric Carle
I Am the King	Natalie Dieterle
I Can Do It	Sarah Albee
I Can't Get My Turtle to Move	Elizabeth Lee O'Donnell
Julius' Candy Corn	Kevin Henkes
Kangaroo Kazoo	Wendy Cheyette Lewison
The Kite	Mary Packard
Love and Kisses	Sara Wilson
Miss Mary Mack	Lori Haskins
Moo Moo Brown Cow	Jakki Wood
My Trucks	Kristen Hall
One Moose, Twenty Mice	Clare Barton
Quick, Quack, Quick	Mary Ann Hoberman
Shanna's Bear Hunt	Jean Marzollo
/l/	
I Like a Snack on an Iceberg	Iris Hiskey Arno
I Love you Sun, I Love you Moon	Karen Pandell
I Need a Lunch Box	Pat Cummings
I See a Leaf	Grace Maccarone
The Lamb Who Loved to Laugh	Carol Puglianon-Martin
Lazy Lion	Mwenye Hadithi
Love, Lola	Dianne DeGroat
Mary Had a Little Lamb	Sarah Hale
My Friends	Taro Gomi
Ten Little Lambs	Alice McGinty

Phonemic Awareness Resources

/m/	
Are you My Mother?	P.D. Eastman
Caps for Sale	Esphyr Slobodkina
Down on the Farm	Greg Scelsa
Hand, Hands, Fingers, Thumb	Al Perkins
Messy Moose	Lois Beck
Monkey's Miserable Monday	Valerie Garfield
Mud	Wendy Cheyette Lewison
Old MacDonald Had a Farm	Amy Schartz
One Moose, Twenty Mice	Clare Barton
Sam and the Firefly	P.D. Eastman
There's a Monster in My House	Stephen Cartwright

/n/	
Barn Cat	Carol Smith
The Best Nest	P.D. Eastman
Monkeys in the Jungle	Angie Sage
The Nicest Newt	Heather Feldman

/p/ and blends	
Beep! Beep!	Barbara George
Can I Help?	Marilyn Jonovitz
Can you Hop?	Lisa Lawson
Dark Night, Sleepy Night	Harriet Ziefert
Hop, Hop, Hop	Ann Whitford Paul
Hop on Pop	Dr. Seuss
Jump Frog, Jump	Robert Kalan

Building Better Readers

A Nap in a Lap	Sarah Wilson
Pierre the Penguin	Jean Marzollo
Piggie Pie Po	Audrey Woods
The Princess and the Pig	Jonathon Emmett
Princess Pigtoria and the Pea	Pamela Duncan Edwards
Polar Babies	Susan Ring
Sheep Follow	Monica Wellingston
Sheep on a Ship	Nancy Shaw
Stomp, Stomp	Bob Kolar
Ten Apples Up on Top	Dr. Seuss
/r/	
The Big Red Sled	Jane Gerver
Dinnertime!	Sue Williams
I Like Red	Robert Bright
My Rhinoceros	Jon Agee
Rain	Manya Stojic
Ravenous Ralph	Julie Brinckloe
Red is Best	Kathy Stinson
Roaring Rockets	Tony Mitton
Roll Over	Merle Peek
Rosie Rabbit's Radish	Wendy Cheyette Lewison
Running Rhino	Mwenye Hadithi
Ten Monsters in a Bed	Rozane Lanczak Williams
Ten Red Apples	Pat Hutchins

Phonemic Awareness Resources

/s/ and blends	
A House for a Mouse	Babs Shook
Anybody at Home?	H.A. Rey
Bear Snores On	Karma Wilson
Boo to a Goose	Mem Fox
Brown Bear, Brown Bear, What Do You See?	Bill Martin
Goose on the Loose	Phillip Roxbee Cox
I Went Walking	Sue Williams
Maisy Goes on a Sleepover	Lucy Cousins
Messy Moose	Lois Bick
Mouse Mess	Linnea Riley
Put Me in the Zoo	Dr. Seuss
Sand	Pam Miller
Seal's Silly Sandwich	Dorothy Sklar
Silly Sally	Audrey Wood
Six Silly Foxes	Alex Moran
Sleepover Mouse	Mary Packard
Some Smug Slug	Pamela Duncan Edwards
Spider on the Floor	Raffi
Six Sleepy Sheep	Judith Ross Enderle
The Very Busy Spider	Eric Carle
/t/ and blends	
Boats	Shane Corey
Cat Games	Harriet Ziefert
Crunch Munch	Jonathan London

Building Better Readers

Harry's Hat	Ann Tompart
I Want a Pet	Barbara Gregorich
Is it Time?	Marilyn Janovitz
Old Hat, New Hat	Stan and Jan Bernstein
Terrific Trains	Brian Mitton
Tricky Tortoise	Mwenye Hadithi
When Tilly Turtle Came to Tea	Carol Pugliano-Martin
/w/	
Walter was Worried	Laura Vacarro Seege
Word Wizard	Catherine Falwell
Worm's Wagon	Samantha Berger
Wild, Wild Wolves	Joyce Milton
/z/	
Buzz	Eileen Spinelli
Greedy Zebra	Mwenye Hadithi
Put Me in the Zoo	Dr. Seuss
Zack the Lazy Zebra	Wendy Cheyette Lewison
/ʃ/	
Never, Ever Shout in a Zoo	Karma Wilson
Shadow	Deanna Calvert
Shapes All Over Town	Victoria Hinkle
Shark in the Park	Phil Roxabee Cox
Sheep Follow	Monica Wellington
Sheep on a Ship	Nancy Shaw

Phonemic Awareness Resources

Shivering Sheep*	Shari Robertson
Shoe Town	Susan Stevens Crummel
Shoo Fly	Iza Trapani
Smiley Shark	Ruth Galloway
Ten Little Fish	Audrey Wood
Where is the Green Sheep?	Mem Fox
/tʃ/	
A Day at the Beach	Mircea Vasiliu
At the Beach	Anne and Harlan Rockwell
Baa Choo	Sarah Weeks
Beach Day	Karen Roosa
Bears at the Beach	Niki Yektai
Chugga-Chugga Choo-Choo	Keven Lewis
Crunch Munch	Jonathan London
I Need a Lunch Box	Pat Cummings
Itchy, Itchy, Chicken Pox	Grade Maccarone
Sea, Sand, Me	Patricia Hubbell
Spot Goes to the Beach	Eric Hill
Which Witch is Which	Pat Hutchins
/dʒ/	
The Giant Jellybean Jar	Marcie Aboff
Jackaloupe	Janet Stevens
Jaguar's Jamboree	Helen Moore
Jump!	Scott Fischer
Jump Frog, Jump!	Robert Kalan

/ə/	
Bears Says Thanks	Karma Wilson
Oh, the Thinks you can Think	Dr. Seuss
This Train	Paul Collicut
BOOKS TARGETING PHONOLOGICAL PROCESSES (AND SOUND PLAY)	
The Bark Park* (Voicing Contrasts)	Elizabeth Redhead Kriston
Go By Goat* (Final Consonant Deletion)	Elizabeth Redhead Kriston
My Cow Can Bow* (Front/Back Contrasts)	Shari Robertson
Pants on Ants* (Initial Consonant Deletion)	Elizabeth Redhead Kriston
Sail By a Tail* (Stopping)	Elizabeth Redhead Kriston

* These books are available from Dynamic Resources

www.dynamic-resources.org

Phonemic Awareness Resources

WEB-BASED RESOURCES FOR BUILDING PHONEMIC AWARENESS

http://www.teams.lacoe.edu/reading/assessments/assessments/html
- screening measures for rhyming, blending, and segmenting.

www.learning by design.com
- Spelling curriculum materials linking to phonemic awareness

http://www.ldonline.og/article/6254
- visual of the steps of Phonological Awareness

http://www.readingrockets.org/article.256/
- Lots of great activities including Elkonen box templates, book suggestions, and more

http://www.auburn.edu/academic/education/reading_genie/
- Lots of great activities and lesson ideas. Try the tongue ticklers!

http://www.auburn.edu/academic/education/reading_genie/mouthmoves.html
- A great resource that provides cues for many sounds in terms of mouth feel, gesture, and meaningful representations.

Example: Phoneme /d/

Mouth Feel	Tip of tongue touches above your top teeth. Voice box on.
Gesture	Knock on table
Meaningful Representation	Door knock.

Phoneme Frog Finger Puppet

Phonemic Awareness Resources

Jump Frog, Jump!

Reproducible For Educational Use-Dynamic Resources

Building Better Readers

Reproducible For Educational Use-Dynamic Resources

PICTURE PIECES

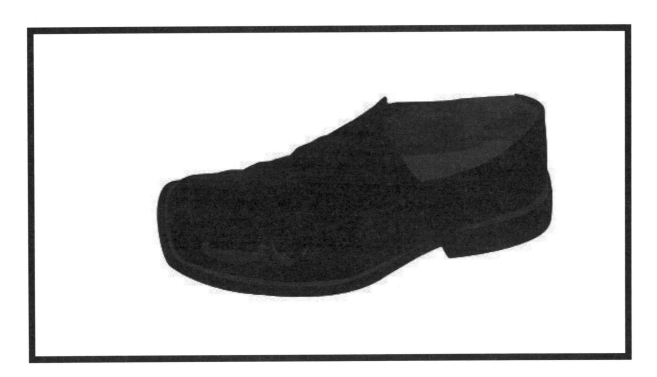

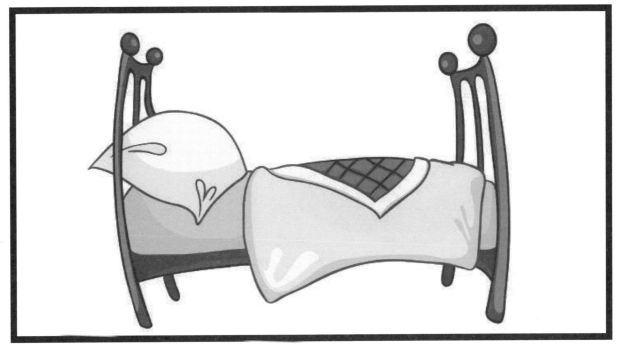

Building Better Readers

Reproducible For Educational Use-Dynamic Resources

Phonemic Awareness Resources

CHAPTER 3

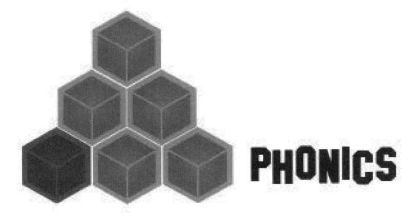

Phonics

Understanding the alphabetic principle—that words are made up of letters and that letters represent sounds—is a critical step in learning to read. **Phonics** is the instructional method used to facilitate this principle. It targets the ==discrete, learned skill of matching a phoneme (sound) with a specific grapheme (letter).== Once children understand that there is a letter code that represents the sounds they hear in words, they are ready to begin matching and memorizing these relationships. It is typically at this point that a parent will proudly announce that their child is "learning to read!"

Of course, we know reading begins LONG before the first word is slowly decoded and hesitantly read, just as we know language learning occurs long before the first word is proudly said. Learning the code and expressing it—either in the oral or written mode—provides an observable, measurable representation of an extremely complex underlying cognitive construct. However, reading or saying a word is only the tip of the linguistic iceberg. In fact, a great deal of the important development that supports the ability to read or talk is essentially invisible.

> *Phonics instruction is not appropriate for children who have not yet developed phonemic/phonological awareness.*

Unfortunately, in some circles, phonics has become the primary focus of instruction rather than a single component. One of the reasons for this is that phonics instruction focuses on a concrete, closed skill set. Since there are a finite number of letters in the alphabet, there are only so many possible relationships between phonemes and graphemes. Once all of these relationships have been mastered and memorized, phonics instruction is essentially complete. As a result, measuring progress related to phonics is fairly straightforward, which, as we know, is highly valued by those who believe that the only learning that is important is that which can be easily quantified.

However, we also know that literacy is primarily a language-based skill that requires a much larger set of skills and competencies than merely matching sounds and symbols—many of which are difficult to pin down using a standardized assessment! Fortunately, by emphasizing that effective reading instruction balances instruction in phonics with a strong program in language enrichment to maximize learning, the National Reading Panel supports what SLPs have known for a long time.

That is not to say that instruction in phonics is unnecessary. To the contrary, research shows that phonics instruction is a key skill in learning to read and instruction related to the alphabetic principle is beneficial to students from K-6th grade (or later if warranted). However, as SLPs, we may need to emphasize to colleagues and parents that formal phonics instruction is neither appropriate nor effective for children who have not yet developed phonemic awareness. Phonics is also NOT the most important, or even the most fundamental skill in learning to read.

Building Better Readers

In fact, for many children who struggle with phonics, the difficulty lies not in an inability to match sounds and symbols, but in a lack of phonemic awareness and/or oral vocabulary deficits.

Our role as speech-language pathologists is not typically one of providing direct phonics instruction to students—nor should it be (we have enough on our plates). Classroom teachers, reading specialists, and teachers of children with learning disabilities are well-trained in phonics instruction. Consequently, children with identified deficits related to phonics are typically provided with effective remediation by one of these very capable professionals. What we can, and should, do is work closely with others to determine if children who are having difficulties learning to read have a more fundamental problem related to the linguistic aspects of literacy. Then, we can systematically address those problems to maximize a student's potential for reading success.

So, while SLPs would most likely not be providing direct phonics instruction as a part of an IEP or clinical intervention plan, we can certainly point out sound-symbol relationships as we work with students on our caseloads. For example, SLPs typically use the grapheme representation rather than the IPA symbol when providing children a visual cue for "their" sound; strengthening both the concept of sound/symbol relationships and the link between that specific letter and the student's targeted sound.

My favorite way of folding practice with phonics into intervention is to incorporate books that target language-based constructs, such as vocabulary and predicting, that also just happen to include opportunities for matching sounds and symbols. This allows me to target the complex linguistic skills that underlie reading while, at the same time, providing indirect learning of the alphabetic principle.

Fortunately, there are a lot of books available that go way beyond the "A is for …." format. I have included description of a few of my favorites here. You can find more in the *Phonics Resources* section that follows.

A Is for Angry: An Animal and Adjective Alphabet (Sandra Boynton)

As is typical from Sandra Boynton, this book is packed with lots of silly critters doing silly things. Pairing each animal with an adjective that starts with the same letter provides a great resource for phonemic awareness and vocabulary building (e.g., the rhinoceros is *rotund*) as well as facilitating an understanding of alphabetic principle. There are also plenty of opportunities for discussion about why the anteater is angry (did he run out of ants? Did he have a bad day?) or the fox is frightened (could it be the flying fish zooming across the top of the page?) or the opossum is outraged (note that the playful pig on the facing page is making fun of him!).

Phonics

Alpha Oops! The Day Z went First (Alethea Kontis)

This is an alphabet book with an attitude! When Z decides that "Zebra and I are SICK of this last-in-line stuff," the entire alphabet gets turned on its ear and a wonderful chaos ensues that is sure to lure in even the most reluctant reader. The letters carry on like spoiled children, jockeying for position, lobbying for a second chance—some even have to take a bathroom break! This book is both entertaining and educational, balancing a sense of playfulness with opportunities for creative thinking. It is also loaded with rich vocabulary and encourages critical thinking as children try to figure out what might happen next. Don't limit this book to your very youngest students—it's also great fun for older kids and adults.

Alphabet City (Stephen Johnson)

Here is another "ABC Book" that is not limited to beginning readers. In fact, I have found that it is an excellent resource for middle elementary all the way through high school. Each letter is depicted using photos of everyday objects and places in New York City. For instance, "A" is represented in the braced end of a construction worker's sawhorse. Graceful "Y"s are formed by dual-headed streetlights that march along a highway. Some letters are obvious and easy to pick out (such as the "E" that is formed by a sideways view of a traffic light), but for others the reader must be willing to look beyond the obvious and discover the connection using small details and imagination.

You can easily extend the concept presented by the author of this book by having students search for letters in their own environments—school, city, home, wherever! This resource is especially good for visual learners, but you will find opportunities to engage students of all ages and ability levels.

✱ **Inspired by this book? Try An A to Z Walk in the Park (R.M. Smith)**

Tomorrow's Alphabet (George Shannon)

This alphabet book engages students by asking them to think ahead and out of the box. For each letter, readers are given a prompt such as "A is for Seed" and then asked to predict what that seed could become "tomorrow" that would actually start with the targeted letter. (Here, "apple."). Some of the tomorrow's alphabet pairs are not too difficult to figure out (*V is for paper, tomorrow's valentine*), but some are a bit trickier (*E is for wood, tomorrow's embers*). This book inspires oral discussion, encourages critical thinking, and builds vocabulary.

Building Better Readers

Museum ABC (The NY Metropolitan Museum of Art)

Everybody knows that A is for apple, but does everybody see an apple in the same way? What better place to look for the answer than in the collections of the Metropolitan Museum of Art, where some of the most interesting apples in the world can be found? Artists from ancient times to the present, and their apples, boats, cats, and representatives of every other letter of the alphabet, provide wonderful opportunities for conversation and critical thinking. For each letter, images are plucked from contrasting works of art, all the same subject, but no two alike. F is for feet, of course, but these feet are found in an Egyptian mural, a Japanese woodcutting print, a Renaissance canvas, and a nineteenth-century French painting.   A little culture can go a long way to help inspire students to learn and grow!

✷ **If you like this book, you might also want to try I Spy: An Alphabet in Art (Lucy Micklethwait)**

Find more books to support language development (and Phonics) in the *Resources* section of this chapter.

PHONICS RESOURCES

Phonics Resources

BOOKS THAT SUPPORT LANGUAGE DEVELOPMENT (AND PHONICS)

A is for Angry: An Animal and Adjective Alphabet	Sandra Boynton
A Isn't for Fox: An Isn't Alphabet	Wendy Ulmer
A is for Ketchup	Xavier Finkley
A My Name is Alice	Jane Bayar
ABC	Eric Carle
Andy: That's My Name	Tomie DePaolo
Alphabears	Kathleen Hague
Alpha Bugs: A Pop-up Alphabet	David Carter
Alphabet City	Stephen Johnson
AlphaOops! The Day Z went First	Alethea Kontis
A-Z	Sandra Boynton
The A-Z Beastly Jamboree	Robert Bender
An A to Z Walk in the Park	R.M. Smith
Brian Wildsmith's ABC	Brian Wildsmith
Eating the Alphabet: Fruit and Vegetables	Lois Ehlert
Farm Alphabet Book	Jane Miller
Hidden Alphabet	Laura Vaccaro Seeger
I Spy: An Alphabet in Art	Lucy Micklethwait
Kippers A to Z: An Alphabet Adventure	Mick Inkpen
Museum ABC	Metropolitan Museum of Art
Q is for Duck	Mary Elting

Building Better Readers

Richard Scarry's Find Your ABC's	Richard Scarry
Tomorrow's Alphabet	George Shannon
The Turn Around, Upside-Down, Alphabet Book	Lisa Campbell Ernest
Z is for Moose	Kelly Bingham
The Z Was Zapped: A Play in Twenty-Six Acts	Chris Van Allsburg

WEB RESOURCES FOR PHONICS

http://www.readwritethink.org
- Many ideas for phonics instruction with a strong language component

CHAPTER 4

Building Better Readers

Reading Fluency

Reading Fluency is often described as the bridge between the lower level processes of reading—such as phonics and decoding—and the higher level process of comprehension. As depicted in the diagram, reading fluency is made up of three key components.

Reading fluency is the ability to read aloud:

➢ with a high degree of accuracy

➢ at an efficient rate, and

➢ with appropriate prosody or expression.

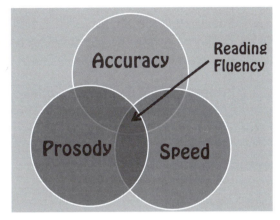

The research indicates that there is a strong correlation between an individual's level of reading fluency and his or her comprehension of what has been read. Fluent readers don't waste cognitive resources on decoding individual words. They can, therefore, focus their attention on making connections between what they are reading and their own background knowledge and experience. In this way, reading fluency maximizes cognitive resources, allowing the reader to concentrate on the *content* of the text, rather than the *form.*

However, very few of us start off as fluent readers. Think about how new readers struggle when asked to read an unknown passage aloud. Their performance is generally marked by long pauses, false starts, a slow pace, and little or no intonation as they struggle to decode each word as they come to it. Questions, statements, or exclamations, typically marked by intonational changes in competent readers, all sound the same (labored!) because the reader is usually not even aware of the type of sentence he or she is reading. I have often suggested that first grade teachers—whose job it is to listen to their students struggle through oral reading day after day—probably deserve some sort of "combat pay!"

In contrast, fluent readers use appropriate intonation, or prosody—such as using a rising intonation at the end of the sentence to signal a question or a falling intonation for statements. High meaning words (e.g., nouns and verbs) are stressed more heavily than words that impact less on the meaning of the sentence (e.g., articles or conjunctions). They have learned when and where to pause and match their reading and breathing to natural breaks in the text. Fluent readers typically have a solid base of age/grade appropriate sight words that allows them to recognize the majority of the words they read automatically. This results in a quick and effortless deliver because the reader does not have to decode each word individually. Consequently, as fluency increases, reading more closely resembles the natural rhythms of a typical conversation resulting in reading that is smooth and easily understood by the listener.

Each of the three components of fluency contributes to text comprehension.

Accuracy: Obviously, misreading words has a negative effect on determining the intended meaning of the text. For example, decoding the word "*garden*" as "*garage*" or "*gargle*" or "*gardenia*" would completely change the meaning of the sentence, *"She was reading in the garden."*

Speed: In addition, an individual who must work hard to decode words sound-by-sound will most likely overtax the cognitive system so that few resources are left over to process the meaning of the text.

Intonation: Finally, readers who are unable to group words into meaningful chunks of information or apply prosodic elements inappropriately also risk misinterpretation of the passage. Conversely, a student who is reading fluently demonstrates that he or she has made the important shift from decoding sound-by-sound (or even word-by-word) through their accurate, rapid, and prosodic oral reading of written material.

READING FLUENCY AND PRAGMATICS

Reading fluency can also provide insight into a student's understanding of the pragmatic aspects of communication. As mentioned previously, written language requires both a sender and a receiver. Because they typically must devote a large proportion of their cognitive resources to decoding, non-fluent readers may miss, or misunderstand, the humor, figurative language, imagination, and drama intended by the author. Conversely, fluent readers demonstrate their knowledge of pragmatics by reading aloud using strategies, such as appropriate prosody, stress, and phrasing, that facilitate comprehension of the passage for their listeners.

THE IMPORTANCE OF PROSODY

Typically, only the components of speed and accuracy are evaluated when assessing reading fluency. This is generally accomplished by asking a student to read a passage aloud while noting decoding errors, timing the passage, and comparing the results to a normed database. However, while this does provide information on reading *automaticity*, it is not an accurate assessment of reading *fluency*.

An over-emphasis on speed over prosody is problematic. In fact, reading too quickly can actually lead to a *decrease* in comprehension of the text—which defeats the whole purpose of reading! So, while speed and accuracy are important, measuring reading fluency on these two parameters alone is counter-productive to facilitating comprehension and literacy development as a whole.

It is important to remember that the end goal, in fact the entire reason, for reading is *comprehension* of the written text. Reading fluency, on the other hand, is NOT an end goal. This key point can be lost in the zeal to improve speed and accuracy of oral reading.

Reading Fluency

While speed and accuracy are mostly a reflection of a students' ability to decode words (lower level processes), students who read aloud with appropriate ***prosody*** demonstrate that they are actively engaged with the actual content of the text. So, by providing students with strategies that target improved prosody, we support the development of reading comprehension.

Classroom teachers and reading specialists typically do an excellent job addressing the speed and accuracy components of reading fluency. SLPs, with a strong knowledge base related to oral language and social communication, are uniquely well-equipped to facilitate the prosodic elements of reading. Further, in most cases, activities that improve reading fluency and prosody can also facilitate improved performance in other language-based disability areas. Consequently, they are appropriate to incorporate into intervention and treatment/educational plans for children with language and literacy delays.

EVALUATING READING FLUENCY - INCLUDING PROSODY

While you can evaluate prosody just by listening to a student read, I personally use the NAEP Oral Reading Fluency Scale as shown on the following page. While it is an informal measure, it assesses all of the components of reading fluency. Further, it is quick, accurate, and extremely helpful to establishing baseline data, the development of appropriate intervention targets, and progress monitoring. Give it a try—I think you'll like it!

FACILITATING READING FLUENCY

As one would predict, studies have shown that many children with oral communication delays are at risk for deficits in the comprehension of both oral and written text. Fortunately, given the already full plate that many SLPs are currently managing, reading fluency can be incorporated into intervention that targets other goals related to communication with minimal effort.

The best way to facilitate reading fluency is to READ! So, you will note that the strategies that follow center around having students read aloud with a primary focus on improving the prosodic component of reading fluency.

Building Better Readers

Score	Criteria
NAEP Oral Reading Fluency Scale	
4	Reads primarily in larger, meaningful phrase groups. Although some regressions, repetitions, and deviations from the text may be present, these do not appear to detract from the overall structure of the story. Preservation of the author's syntax is consistant. Some or most of the story is read with expressive interpretation. Reads at an appropriate rate.
3	Reads primarily in three- and four-word phrase groups. Some smaller groupings may be present. However, the majority of phrasing seems appropriate and preserves the syntax of the author. Little or no expressive interpretation is present. Reader attempts to read expressively and some of the story is read with expression. Generally reads at an appropriate rate.
2	Reads primarily in two-word phrase groups with some three- and four-word groupings. Some word-by-word reading may be present. Word groupings may seem awkward and unrelated to the larger context of the sentence or passage. A small portion of the text is read with expressive interpretation. Reads significant sections of the text excessively slow or fast.
1	Reads primarily word-by-word. Occasional two-word or three-word phrases may occur - but these are infrequent and/or they do not preserve meaningful syntax. Lacks expresive interpretation. Reads text excesssively slow. A score of "1" should also be given to a student who reads with excessive speed, ignoring punctuation and other phrase boundaries, and reads with little or no expression.

SOURCE: US Department of Education, Institute of Educational Sciences, National Center for Educational Statistics, National Assessment of Educational Progress (NAEP), 2002 Oral Reading Study. Accessible at: nces.ed.gov/nationsreportcard/studies/ors/scale.asp

STRATEGIES FOR BUILDING
READING FLUENCY

REPEATED ORAL READINGS

One of the most studied methods of increasing reading fluency is to read the same passage aloud multiple times. Often called repeated oral readings, this strategy enhances skill in all aspects of reading fluency: speed, accuracy, and prosody. Reading the same passage aloud numerous times allows the reader to concentrate on lower level decoding, such as sounding out words or identifying individual word meanings, on the first reading trials. Once this information is processed, the reader can then direct his or her attention to reading fluently and discerning text meaning.

How many times would you practice a reading passage that you knew you were going to read aloud in a high-stress or high-profile situation? You certainly would not go into it "cold" without several run-throughs to help you feel the rhythm of the passage, practice any words that might be a bit tricky to roll off your tongue, and to make sure you understand the content of the passage.

The National Reading Panel found that typical readers need to read a passage four times to reach maximum fluency levels. Less competent readers will need substantially more practice reading the passage aloud to reach the same level of fluency than those with more typical reading skills. While studies have not yet determined the ideal number of repetitions necessary for achieving reading fluency for weaker readers, the general consensus, as reflected in the quote in the sidebar, is the more times the better. Obviously, more difficult passages will require more readings.

> Re-reading a text seven times is better than three times which is better than one time.
>
> Chard et al., 2002

Thus, reading the passage aloud numerous times helps the reader master all of the elements of the task more effectively—and fluently! (It is important to note here that reading a passage silently has not been shown to lead to significant increases in reading fluency.) Ideally, because the goal is to help the children become more fluent readers, passages that are at, or slightly below, students' current reading levels should be chosen for practice.

Using text that is part of the student's classroom curriculum for repeated oral reading is a relatively effortless way of connecting intervention/remediation to the classroom setting. Multiple readings of a passage prior to its introduction in the classroom can facilitate better overall comprehension of the topic (which can facilitate more active participation in the classroom). Of course, prior arrangements regarding a specific passage that your student will be responsible for reading aloud in class is an ideal way to enhance skill development and bolster confidence.

MODEL FLUENT READING

Empirical studies have repeatedly suggested that listening to proficient readers who model an appropriate pace and prosody can facilitate the listener's reading fluency. However, while simply reading aloud to children is beneficial, there are a number of even more powerful strategies that provide multiple opportunities for hearing and producing fluent reading. In fact, children do not actually have to be at the formal reading stage to begin to learn about reading fluently.

Echo Reading is effective in facilitating reading fluency in even very young children. When using this strategy, the adult reads a short passage and then invites the child to "Say what I say" or "Copy me," encouraging the child to repeat what the adult has read. This provides an opportunity for children to experience reading fluency even before they have reached the formal stages of reading instruction Since Echo Reading does not require children to actually decode the words, they are free to concentrate on the prosodic elements of the story. As with most interventions, the earlier children have the opportunity to practice reading fluency, the more apt they are to become fluent readers once they actually begin to independently decode words.

In **Paired Reading**, the adult models appropriate phrasing, rate, and prosody and the child or student contributes by chiming in as he or she is able to complete the rhyme, sentence, or page. This strategy can be used with children who are already decoding words or with younger children who have heard the story read aloud several times prior to asking them to join in. This is a very natural strategy for most adults, but its value to developing fluent readers is not generally understood or appreciated. Paired reading is particularly effective when books have a strong rhythm and rhyme or a repetitive phrase that the child can read (or say) each time it appears.

> **Find books that support Echo and Paired Reading in the *Resources* section of this chapter.**

Older children who are still struggling with reading fluency (and other issues related to oral and written language) can also benefit from participating in echo and paired reading with a more capable reader. The key difference is in the materials that are chosen. As with repeated oral readings, books or text passages used in the classroom can be echo or pair read as a way to increase comprehension of the material. If the child will be expected to read the text aloud in class, using paired or echo reading can facilitate a more successful, fluent reading experience.

PROGRESSIVE STORIES

The use of a variety of literature genres is both motivating and beneficial to increasing fluency through repeated oral readings. However, one genre that I find particularly useful is progressive stories which, by their very nature, have repeated readings of the same material built right in. The story is begun with a sentence or two (*This is the house that Jack built*) and an additional part of the story is added each time a page is turned (*This is the door on the house that Jack built*). The story becomes more and more complex as it unfolds, but the reader is only reading a little bit more "new" material each time the page is turned.

Typically, progressive stories also include a lot of natural opportunities to practice phrasing and expression as the story builds and the child becomes more and more familiar with the structure of the text. Start with simpler stories, such as *The Jacket I Wear in the Snow,* and progress to those that include more difficult text and more sophisticated vocabulary (e.g., *Jack's Garden*).

> **See the *Resources* section of this chapter for suggested progressive story books as well as other resources for building reading fluency.**

UNDERSTANDING SENTENCE STRESS

It's worth repeating—prosody is a key component of reading fluency and contributes to the development of good comprehension skills. So, how does sentence stress contribute to prosody and, eventually, reading comprehension?

> Consider the sentence: ***"They are riding horses."***

Stressing "*riding*" or "*horses*" in the sentence makes a big difference in interpretation, signaling whether people are sitting on horses' backs, or the horses are meant for riding rather than pulling a cart or some other purpose. In fact, where the stress is placed in this sentence determines whether "*riding*" is a verb or an adjective.

Most children learn to use, and interpret, appropriate sentence stress without even being aware that they are doing so. However, this may not be true for children who struggle to process language. In fact, they may be completely unaware of the meanings they communicate through their use of stress as well as what stress conveys when used by others. Consequently, explicitly teaching children who struggle with reading about the role of stress in sentences has the potential to help them improve their reading fluency and comprehension (both oral and written).

The following activity introduces students to stress and its impact on sentence meanings:

Method

- ☐ Adult reads sentences aloud and guides student/s in identifying the most important words (those that provide the most information about what each sentence is about).

- ☐ EXAMPLES

    > **Don't** do it!

    > I bought a **dress**.

    > I **hate** mashed potatoes.

    > The party is **tomorrow**!

- ☐ Then, have the student/s read the sentences aloud using the correct stress after following your model.

- ☐ You might also have the student try stressing the WRONG words (e.g., articles) or try reading the sentences with no stress at all (almost impossible) to really get the feel of why stress is so important.

FUN WITH SENTENCE STRESS

The goal of this activity is to have the student/s read a sentence multiple times in response to a specific question stressing a different word in the sentence each time to more accurately communicate meaning. Although not required, I generally look for a picture that can be used to provide a visual cue.

> *This is one of my FAVORITE go-to strategies for improving reading prosody.*

An additional advantage of this activity is that it includes a built-in repeated oral readings component since the student has a chance to read the sentence numerous times. As the text becomes more familiar, more attention can be allocated to the meanings expressed rather than to decoding the words.

Method

- ☐ Find a picture that depicts an action or attribute or some other interesting detail.

- ☐ Construct a sentence that describes the picture. Ideally, it should have, at a minimum, a subject, verb, and a direct object.

- ☐ Next, have the student read the sentence aloud.

- ☐ The student then reads the sentence again in response to a series of questions, stressing the appropriate word to most accurately answer each question. For example:

> **Tony is walking in the rain.**

✹ Who is walking in the rain?
  o *"**Tony** is walking in the rain."*

✹ What is Tony doing in the rain?
  o *"Tony is **walking** in the rain."*

✹ Where is Tony walking?
  o *"Tony is walking in the **rain**."*

Building Better Readers

It's even more fun when you use funny pictures:

> **The sheep is eating the book.**

* Who is eating the book?
    o "The **sheep** is eating the book."

* What is the sheep doing with the book?
    o "The sheep is **eating** the book."

* What is the sheep eating?
    o "The sheep is eating the **book**."

> **The cow is wearing high heels.**

* Who is wearing high heels?
    o *"The **cow** is wearing high heels."*

* What is the cow wearing?
    o *"The cow is wearing high **heels**."*

* What is the cow doing with the high heels?
    o *"The cow is **wearing** high heels."*

* What kind of heels is the cow wearing?
    o *"The cow is wearing **high** heels."*

Reading Fluency

Variations/Extensions

- ❖ This is a great large group activity. Students love to chant the responses aloud, stressing the appropriate word with gusto.

- ❖ To up the fun factor, invite the students to bring in funny (appropriate) pictures or photos.

- ❖ Next, have students create, and then ask, the questions that go with the pictures.

- ❖ Newspaper headings can be mined for this exercise as well! Here's a headline from my local newspaper on August 5, 2012.

➢ NASA Spacecraft Speeding Toward Landing on Mars

- ✹ What is speeding toward Mars?
    - o *"**NASA spacecraft** is speeding toward landing on Mars."*

- ✹ Where will the spacecraft land?
    - o *"NASA spacecraft is speeding toward landing on **Mars**."*

- ✹ What will the spacecraft do when it gets to Mars?
    - o *"NASA spacecraft is speeding toward **landing** on Mars."*

- ✹ How is the spacecraft moving toward Mars?
    - o *"NASA spacecraft is **speeding** toward landing on Mars."*

POETRY (AND PUNCTUATION)

Poetry can help readers develop a broad range of fluency skills and provides concentrated practice with rhythm, cadence, expression, and prosody. You can use poetry written by others or work with the child to help him or her write their own poetic masterpieces.

As noted in the title of this strategy, to target prosody, you may need to take time to explicitly teach students how punctuation and reading aloud go together. Good readers typically learn this without explicit instruction, but struggling readers often do not. So, take time to demonstrate that a question mark at the end of a sentence should be accompanied by a rising intonation; a period, a falling intonation and a long pause; a comma, a short pause.

Here is a portion of a poem I wrote for my students for reading fluency practice (among other things). Note that there is punctuation to signal prosody, strong rhythm and rhyme, and a silly story that makes it fun to read. (The full poem can be found in the *Resources* section of this chapter)

> *My brother eats bugs?*
>
> *My brother eats bugs!*
>
> *My horrid and horrible brother eats bugs!*
>
> *He says they're delicious, and also nutritious,*
>
> *And wants me to try one, but I'm too suspicious.*
>
> *Big black ants, little tiny fleas,*
>
> *Wings and antennae, he downs them with ease.*
>
> *Crunchy or squishy, fluttery or swishy,*
>
> *He says they taste yummy, but something sounds fishy.*
>
> *Grasshoppers, dragonflies, termites, and slugs*
>
> *My horrid and horrible brother eats bugs!*

Shel Silverstein's books of poetry (See *Resources* section of this chapter) are particularly good for practice with reading fluency—and will keep the interest of most students even into middle school. Readers can choose from short, one-paragraph poems to those that are several pages in length. They are great for choral reading as well. (Unfortunately, I cannot reprint any of Silverstein's poems in this resources due to copyright restrictions—but do check them out!)

Reading Fluency

Here's another offering from poet Alfred Noyes that provides opportunities to improve reading fluency AND enrich students' vocabularies.

Daddy Fell into the Pond

Everyone grumbled. The sky was grey.
We had nothing to do and nothing to say.
We were nearing the end of a dismal day,
And then there seemed to be nothing beyond,
Then Daddy fell into the pond!

And everyone's face grew merry and bright,
And Timothy danced for sheer delight.
"Give me the camera, quick, oh quick!
He's crawling out of the duckweed!" Click!

Then the gardener suddenly slapped his knee,
And doubled up, shaking silently,
And the ducks all quacked as if they were daft,
And it sounded as if the old drake laughed.
Oh, there wasn't a thing that didn't respond
When
Daddy fell into the pond!

Reprinted by permission of the Society of Authors as the Literary Representative of the Estate of Alfred Noyes.

SONGS AND CHANTS

Songs and chants—particularly those that call for physical participation at various points—are an excellent way to develop the rhythm and cadence of fluent reading. To illustrate the power of a chant in terms of promoting prosody, try saying the alphabet without lapsing into the familiar sing-song rhythm that most of us learned at an early age. You'll find it takes quite a bit more effort to say each letter without expression than to just sing it!

The same thing happens when you read a book that is based on an already-known song or chant. The prosodic elements are already embedded into your long-term memory, which aids in a delivery that is rich in prosody and intonation. There are a number of books available that are written around songs or chants that can be particularly effective in linking oral and reading fluency. Here are some examples (you can find more in the *Resources* section of this chapter).

I Ain't Gonna Paint No More (Karen Beaumont)

Based on the song "It Ain't Gonna Rain No More," the rhythmic text of this fantastic book can be either read or sung with equal effectiveness. When Mama catches her son "paintin' pictures on the floor/and the ceiling/and the walls/and the curtains/and the door," she sticks him in the tub and declares, "Ya ain't a-gonna paint no more!" Not to be deterred, the child rescues his hidden supplies and proceeds to paint himself from head to toe. As he adds gobs of paint to different body parts, he accompanies his work with rhyming lyrics such as, "*So I take some red/ and I paint my..../**HEAD**!*" and "*Aw, what the heck! Gonna paint my..../**NECK**!*" The farther you go, the more body parts are covered until, when you think that the boy has painted everything, he finishes with, "*But I'm such a nut,/gonna paint my.../**WHAT?!***" Fortunately, he's out of supplies and winds up back in the bathtub.

Since the last word of each verse comes on the following page, readers get the satisfaction of completing the anticipated rhyme and seeing each newly painted body part with every page turned. Also, the author splashes color all over, uses white space cleverly, and includes playful flourishes, such as a marching row of ants on the boy's arm and Easter egg designs on his leg. Elongated figures and exaggerated expressions match the silly tone of the story, and the concerned dog who observes the antics is particularly amusing.

Reading Fluency

Take Me Out of the Bathtub (Alan Katz)

In the grand tradition of song parodies like "On Top of Spaghetti," Alan Katz sets funny lyrics to well-known tunes. For instance, a boy (who happens to be wearing roller skates) expresses—to the tune of Take Me Out to the Ballgame— that he has been soaking way too long as he proclaims, *"I've used one, two, three bars of soap/ Take me out... I'm clean!"*

Other amusing entries include "I've Been Cleaning Up My Bedroom" sung to "I've Been Working on the Railroad", and *"Oh give me a break/`Cause I made a mistake/And my library book's overdue"* to the tune of "Home on the Range." "Go, Go, Go to Bed" depicts an exhausted mom slumped in a chair with toys and a child literally bouncing off the ceiling above her. The watercolor illustrations are equally entertaining, with exaggerated features and situations giving them a cartoon look.

✷ **If you like this book, try "I'm Still Here in the Bathtub," also by Alan Katz.**

Mary Wore her Red Dress (and Henry Wore his Green Sneakers) (Merle Peek)

Using only the words of a folk song as the text, which readers chant as they progress, the story of Katie Bear's birthday party is told through the illustrations. The story begins as a two-page illustrated spread in black and white except for the red dress that is worn by Mary Squirrel and the words: *"Mary wore her red dress, red dress, red dress, Mary wore her red dress all day long."* Flashes of green show up on the next pages as Henry Raccoon joins Mary and the verse changes to *"Henry wore his green sneakers, green sneakers, green sneakers, Henry wore his green sneakers all day long."*

The revelry at the gathering is heightened by Katie's yellow sweater and the blue, purple, orange, etc., in the guests' costumes. Standout details include the Bears' formal garden in bloom, status-symbol house furnishing (marble statues of twin bears flank the fireplace and support the mantel), an imposing birthday cake, and lots of mischief by the party-goers.

The Seals on the Bus (Lenny Hort)

This is a parody of the classic fingerplay "The wheels on the bus go round and round." However, here the seals on the bus go *eerrp, eerrp, eerrpp* (so FUN to make the seal sound while clapping one's forearms together!) and the vipers on the bus go *hiss, hiss, hiss*. Finally, the people on the bus go *help, help, help* and run off the bus, leaving it to an entire menagerie of animals who apparently appreciate mass transportation.

CHORAL READING AND DUET READING

Research suggests that students can improve their fluency skills by reading along with a group of readers or with a single, strong reader as a partner.

In *choral reading*, a group of students read aloud together from the same selection. The teacher or SLP can read along to set the pace and model targeted skills. Choral reading can be as simple as students reading in unison from a single text passage to something quite complicated with different parts of the passage read in different ways. For example, alternate lines might be read more softly or more quickly, at a higher or lower pitch, or by a sub-group of readers.

When less-fluent readers participate in choral reading, they hear and experience the way classmates use pauses, intonations, and stress to give the piece more meaning. Choral reading can be a powerful and motivating technique to improve reading fluency for students with and without identified communication problems and is particularly easy to implement for SLPs who provide any amount of classroom-based intervention.

In *duet reading*, a stronger reader is paired with a less-fluent reader (generally, the stronger reader is an adult). The stronger reader sets the pace and may provide visual tracking by moving his or her finger below each word as it is read in unison. This also provides an opportunity for the weaker reader to experience reading fluency following the lead of a more accomplished reader. To support reading fluency, duet reading can be implemented in a small-group, in one-on-one sessions, or by parents in the home environment.

> **Find books and websites that build reading fluency in the *Resources* section of this chapter.**

Reading Fluency

PARTNER PRACTICE

This activity provides students with opportunities to be both the sender and the receiver in the reading process. This particular variation is set up for pairs of students, but you can adapt this activity for use with larger groups as well.

Method

- ☐ Students decide who will be the **reader** and who will be the **listener.**

- ☐ The **Reader** reads a selection of text aloud three times while the **listener** listens.

- ☐ Listener records his/her observations regarding accuracy, speed, and prosody after the second and third readings using the checklist below (or create your own version).

- ☐ Switch roles and repeat!

Partner Practice!

Here's How My Partner Improved

After the 2nd Reading	After the 3rd Reading	
☐	☐	Remembered more words
☐	☐	Read more smoothly
☐	☐	Read more quickly
☐	☐	Read with more expression

Reader's Name _____

Reading Passage _____

My Name _____

A full-sized, reproducible version of this activity sheet is available in the Resources section of this chapter.

Building Better Readers

BOOKS ON TAPE
(or CD or I-pod or whatever new technology comes along!)

Use of recorded books is an empirically-supported way to facilitate more fluent reading. This strategy provides both a model of fluent reading and opportunities to read along in a form of duet-reading. The evidence provides clear support for the use of this strategy for students in primary through the middle grades. It is also useful for students who are English Language Learners.

There are numerous commercially-available, pre-recorded books as well as websites that provide access to audio-recorded stories. (See the *Resources* section of this chapter for some suggestions). In addition, you can create your own "books on tape" library with little more than an inexpensive audio recorder and a favorite book. (Hint: senior citizens are often happy to help out with this task.)

Recalling that the purpose is to encourage the weaker reader to read along, the audio-recorded reader should set a somewhat slower pace, use short natural phrasing, and a good deal of expression (prosody). Choosing books with interesting characters and engaging storylines facilitates reader attention and the potential for positive benefit .

Hank the Cowdog (John Erickson)

I can't talk about the use of books on tape without referencing one of my favorite series. The stories are set on a cattle ranch in Texas and are narrated by our hero, Hank, who is the self-proclaimed "Head of Ranch Security". Hank believes he is an invaluable part of ranch life, but most of the time he just gets himself in trouble. The cast of characters is rich and diverse (e.g., Wallace and Junior who are buzzards, Drover, Hank's cowardly sidekick, and a pack of coyotes whom Hank refers to as "cannibals.") The stories are read by the author and his wife who play all the characters to perfection.

The chapters are short, the vocabulary is rich, the stories are hilarious, and they are ALL available in audio-recorded form. Hank and I have convinced many a reluctant reader (my own son included) that reading can actually be a positive experience. You can find out more about Hank at his website www.hankthecowdog.com. Happy trails!

Reading Fluency

YOU OUGHTA BE IN PICTURES!

Reading and acting out movie and TV scripts provides a legitimate, or "real" reason to read and re-read text as students rehearse and prepare to act out the story or script for others This activity also promotes active engagement (important for comprehension) and is highly motivating for most students (an essential part of a becoming a strong reader).

I have had very positive responses to this activity—and it's even better when students can practice reading fluency using scripts from their personal favorite movies and TV shows. In effect, they have had the lines modeled by the original actors and they can try to imitate the delivery when they read it (although it may be a bit difficult to match James Earl Jones' delivery of "May the force be with you" or Forest Gump's "Life is like a box of chocolates," it's fun to try!)

Where to find these scripts, you ask? Head on over to Drew's Script-O-Rama (www.script-o-rama.com) where you can find scripts for virtually EVERY movie and TV show ever made. (Be sure to click on the picture in the upper right hand corner to enter the actual website). This website is continually updated with new information and resources. Give it a try!

DREW'S-SCRIPT-O-RAMA
www.script-o-rama.com

READING FLUENCY RESOURCES

BOOKS FOR ECHO READING

Across the Stream	Mirra Ginsburg
Bears in Pairs	Niki Yekai
Bones, Bones, Dinosaur Bones	Byron Barton
Chugga-Chugga-Choo-Choo	Kevin Lewis
Dinner Time!	Jan Pienkowski
Dinosaur Roar	Paul and Henrietta Strickland
Down By the Bay	Raffi
I Went Walking	Sue Williams
In the Small, Small, Pond	Denise Fleming
One Afternoon	Yumi Heo
One Fish, Two Fish, Red Fish, Blue Fish	Dr. Seuss
Pizza Party	Grace Maccarone
Quick As A Cricket	Audrey Wood
Rosie's Walk	Pat Hutchins
Slower Than A Snail	Anne Schreiber
Tidy Titch	Pat Hutchins

BOOKS FOR PAIRED READING

Bear on a Bike	Stella Blackstone
Bear Snores On	Karma Wilson
The Bus for Us	Suzanne Bloom
Buz	Richard Egielski
The Cow Buzzed	Andrea Zimmerman
The Cow that Went Oink	Bernard Most
Don't Forget the Bacon	Pat Hutchins
Each Peach, Pear, Plum	Janet Ahlberg
The Happy Hippopatomi	Betsy Everitt
Hilda Must Be Dancing	Karma Wilson
Jump, Frog, Jump	Robert Kaplan
The Missing Tarts	B. G. Hennessy
One Duck Stuck	Phyllis Root
Pigs A Plenty, Pigs Galore	David McPhail
Silly Sally	Audrey Wood
Where is the Green Sheep?	Mem Fox
Who Stole the Cookies?	Judy Moffatt

Reading Fluency Resources

PROGRESSIVE STORIES

The Cake that Mack Ate	Rose Robart
Drummer Hoff	Barbara Emberly
Fat Frogs on a Skinny Log	Sara Riches
A Frog in the Bog	Karma Wilson
In a Napping House	Audrey Wood
Jack's Garden	Henry Cole
The Mouse that Jack Built	Cyndy Szekeres
The Little Old Lady Who Wasn't Afraid of Anything	Linda Williams
One Fine Day	Nonny Hogrogian
This is the House that Jack Built	Simms Taback
This is the House that was Tidy and Neat	Teri Sloat
The Jacket I Wear in the Snow	Shirley Neitzel

POETRY BOOKS

Antarctic Antics: A Book of Penguin Poems	Judy Sierra
The Armpit of Doom: Funny Poems for Kids	Kenn Nesbitt
Behold the Bold Umprellephant	Jack Prelutsky
Bow Wow Meow Meow: It's Rhyming Cats and Dogs	Douglas Florian
Daffy Down Dillies: Silly Limericks	Edward Lear
A Giraffe and a Half	Shel Silverstein
Falling Up	Shel Silverstein
Fast and Slow: Poems for Advanced Children and Beginning Parents	John Ciardi
For Laughing Out Loud	Jack Prelutsky
Flamingos on the Roof: Poems and Paintings	Calef Brown
Hamsters, Shells, and Spelling Bees	Lee Bennet Hopkins
Hot Dinners: Silly Poems for Kids	Jude Allman
If You're Not Here, Please Raise Your Hand	Kalli Dakos
In the Spin of Things: Poetry in Motion	Rebecca Kai Dotlich
It's Raining Pigs and Noodles	Jack Pelutsky
I Saw You in The Bathtub	Alvin Schwartz
Just Kidding: Funny Poems for Kids	Martin Pierce

Reading Fluency Resources

Kids Pick the Funniest Poems	Bruce Lansky
The Llama Who Had No Pajamas	Mary Ann Hoberman
A Light in the Attic	Shel Silverstein
The New Kid on the Block	Jack Prelutsky
No More Homework! No More Tests! Kids Favorite Funny School Poems	Bruce Lansky
Mirror, Mirror: A Book of Reversible Verse	Marilyn Singer
Once I Laughed My Socks Off	Steve Attewell
Pizza, Pigs, and Poetry	Jack Prelutsky
Poems to Annoy your Parents	Susie Gibbs
Something Big Has Been Here	Jack Prelutsky
There's a Zoo in Room 22	Judy Sierra
Tickets to Ride: An Alphabetic Amusement	Mark Rogalski
Where the Sidewalk Ends	Shel Silverstein

BOOKS FOR CHANTS, RHYMES, AND SONGS

The Ants Go Marching	Jeffery Scherer (and others)
Are you Quite Polite?	Jack Katz
Classic Jump Rope Rhymes, The School-Yard All-Stars Schoolyard Rhymes, Kids' Own Rhymes for Rope-Skipping, Hand Clapping, Ball Bouncing and Just Plain Fun	Klutz Press
Hand, Hand, Fingers, Thumb	P.D. Eastman
I Ain't Gonna Paint No More	Karen Beaumont
I'm Still Here in the Bathtub: Brand New Silly Dilly Songs	Alan Katz
Marsupial Sue	John Lithgow
Mary Wore Her Red Dress	Merle Peek
Miss Mary Mack	Mary Anne Hoberman
Over in the Jungle: A Rainforst Rhyme	Marianne Berkes
Over in the Meadow	Olive Wadsworth
Shoo Fly	Iza Trapani
Skip to My Lou	Mary Ann Hoberman
Take Me Out of the Bathtub and Other Silly Dilly Songs	Alan Katz
Ten in the Bed	Anne Geddes
There were Monkeys in my Kitchen!	Sheree Fitch

Reading Fluency Resources

WEB-BASED RESOURCES FOR BUILDING READING FLUENCY

http://www.gigglepoetry.com
- my favorite resource for poetry theatre. Lots of other poetry-related activities as well.

www.jackprelutsky.com
- the author's personal website. Some fun poems to read aloud.

www.shelsilverstein.com
- activities, poems, and background information about everyone's favorite chidren's poet.

www.poetry4kids.com/
- Ken Nesbitt's poetry site full of funny poems, poetry lessons, poetry games and more.

www.childrenspoetrybookshelf.co.uk/
- lots of poems and fun stuff for kids.

www.hankthecowdog.com
- website for all things Hank. Not to be missed!

http://lightupyourbrain.com/stories/
- lots of great activities for kids, including free audiobooks.

http://www.booksshouldbefree.com/genre/Children
- free audio book downloads for children.

www.script-o-rama.com
- every movie and TV script you can imagine. Just the thing for motivating those reluctant readers to practice stress and intonation!

Building Better Readers

My Brother Eats Bugs

My brother eats bugs?

My brother eats bugs!

My horrid and horrible brother eats bugs!

He says they're delicious, and also nutritious,

And wants me to try one, but I'm too suspicious.

Beetles by the bunch, he crunches for lunch.

Crickets and lice are better with rice.

Big black ants,

Little tiny fleas,

Wings and antennae, he downs them with ease.

I say bugs are icky, he says I'm too picky,

As he gulps down a weevil that makes his chin sticky.

Crunchy or squishy,

Fluttery or swishy.

He says they taste yummy, but something sounds fishy.

Grasshoppers, dragonflies, termites, and slugs,

My horrid and horrible brother eats bugs!

~Shari Robertson ©

Reading Fluency Resources

Partner Practice!

Here's How My Partner Improved

After the 2nd Reading	After the 3rd Reading	
☐	☐	Remembered more words
☐	☐	Read more smoothly
☐	☐	Read more quickly
☐	☐	Read with more expression

Reader's Name _____

Reading Passage _____

My Name _____

Comments:

CHAPTER 5

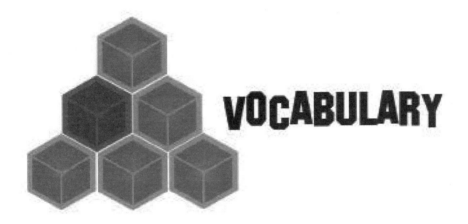

Vocabulary

> "Good readers comprehend more words than poorer readers."
>
> ●●●●●●●●●●●●
>
> ~National Literacy Panel

The evidence is clear. **Vocabulary** plays a critical role in learning to read. After evaluating decades of research related to literacy, the National Reading Panel used the quote noted in the sidebar to sum up their findings. This is not exactly new information to speech-language pathologists who have long understood the critical role of a strong oral vocabulary base to support written language and academic success. (The first time I read this pithy statement, my admittedly adolescent reaction was to roll my eyes and say "duh!").

When I was in high school, I recall my mom, who was an early pioneer in our field, creating what we now call semantic webs for her students on the dining room table after dinner. She also spent a lot of time developing activities to help students figure out words they DIDN'T know using information that they DID know. (I won't reveal how many decades ago this was, but I was most likely wearing my bell bottom jeans and tie-dyed tee-shirt.) At the time, I thought she was some sort of genius for literally drawing her students a map of how to organize and think about vocabulary. Now, we have a robust literature base that supports what my SLP mom understood intuitively—that students need to have a strong foundation of vocabulary for reading and writing.

Fundamentally, to be effective readers, students must be able to make sense of the word they SEE (reading vocabulary) by comparing it to the words they have HEARD (oral vocabulary). In other words, readers must understand the oral meaning of a word before they can comprehend the written version.

In fact, there is a synergistic relationship between and amongst vocabulary development and several of the other key areas identified by the National Reading Panel as critical to reading success. For example, the evidence suggests that children who have strong oral vocabularies more easily learn to identify the individual sounds that make up words (phonemic awareness). Vocabulary knowledge is also linked to decoding. Children learn to map the spoken sounds of a word to its written form with less effort when the word is already a part of their oral vocabulary. So, they can more easily sound out and read the word when they already understand its oral meaning.

However, it is important to emphasize that although phonemic awareness is a strong predictor of success in learning to read, vocabulary is the best predictor of comprehension in the later grades (National Reading Panel Report, 2000). By third grade, many children can read words, but they fail to understand what they read due to vocabulary limitations. In fact, Beimiller (2012) found a strong predictive relationship between vocabulary proficiency in first grade and reading comprehension in 11th grade. This relationship is transparent to most SLPs who understand that to construct meaning from written language, students need to have an adequate vocabulary base as well as a set of strategies to establish the meanings of unknown words from context.

Word Consciousness

As we discuss ways to develop vocabulary, it is important to keep in mind that regardless of age, grade, or ability level, our primary goal should be to help our students become **word conscious**. That is, we want our students to develop an awareness and interest in words and their meanings and to understand and harness the power of words.

Word conscious students enjoy words and are eager to learn words and use them in everyday contexts. They look for opportunities to expand their vocabularies by learning new words as well as new meanings or new ways to use words they already know.

Unfortunately, many students with language and/or literacy difficulties (and a good number of those without identified disability areas) have not developed this trait or, even worse, it has been "taught out" of them by well-meant, but poorly planned, instruction. For instance, despite overwhelming evidence to the contrary, some educators continue to believe that having students look up definitions of words from a prescribed list is an effective way to teach vocabulary. It is not. We will talk more about effective and ineffective methods of vocabulary instruction after a brief review of typical vocabulary development.

> "Word Conscious students are eager to learn new words and use them in everyday contexts."
>
> ~National Reading Panel

Typical Vocabulary Development

For many children, vocabulary learning seems to develop effortlessly and follows a predictable sequence. Around the time typically developing infants celebrate their first birthdays, they recognize a number of words in connected speech and are beginning to produce their first words. By 30 months or so, they have experienced a virtual vocabulary explosion and can produce hundreds of words. These toddlers have also discovered that there are different kinds of words and have begun to combine them using both semantic and syntactic rules.

By the time typically developing children enter Kindergarten, they have acquired a vocabulary of 2000—3000 words. By the end of second grade, we expect children to have a minimum of 6000 distinct words in their vocabularies and to add approximately 3000—3500 words each year they are in school. By the end of high school, students are expected to have learned an astonishing 40,000 to 80,000 words (Stahl, 1999).

Vocabulary

CLASSIFYING VOCABULARY

I find it useful to consider vocabulary tiers, as described by Beck, McKeown, & Kucan (2002), when developing intervention to facilitate word knowledge. Using this framework, vocabulary is divided into groups, or tiers, based on the descriptive value of the words.

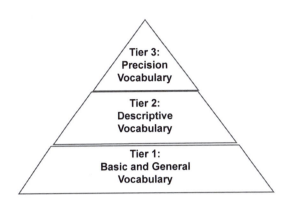

Tier 1. As shown in the graphic, the first tier is the largest and consists of the basic building block words that make up a language. These words are typically well-known and used with a high level of frequency by native speakers of a specific language. In English there are an estimated 8000 word families included in this tier. Tier 1 words rarely require direct instruction for most language learners. While these words are critically important to oral and written language competence, they do not convey specific information. Basic nouns, verbs, adjectives, and what are typically referred to as "sight words" are found in this tier.

Tier 2. Tier 2 words provide more detail and specificity than those found in Tier 1 and occur across a variety of environments. These words are used with a high level of frequency in adult language and literature and are extremely important to both reading and writing. Tier 2 words more accurately express feelings, emotions, and information; however, they may have multiple meanings and still leave room for interpretation by the listener. Tier 2 words are an appropriate focus for direct instruction techniques because they have a powerful impact on both oral and written language. In addition, they are good indicators of progress in the academic curriculum. There are approximately 7000 families that make up Tier 2 in English.

Tier 3. The third tier, the smallest, is made up of words which are typically described as "precision" vocabulary. These are low-frequency words that evoke a specific image or concept. Tier 3 words are most often associated with specific field of study or school subjects (e.g., biology, chemistry) or with particular occupations, hobbies, or dialects. Tier 3 words can be especially tricky for adolescents who are struggling with academic vocabulary.

> **Sample Vocabulary Words by Tier**
>
> ● ● ● ● ● ● ● ● ● ● ● ● ● ● ●
>
> **Tier 1**
> *drink, car, laugh, girl, sad, jump, blue, big, puppy, apple, smile, sing, table, cheek, listen, baby*
>
> **Tier 2**
> *icon, create, branching, fortunate, merchant, endure, varmint, maintain, vehicle*
>
> **Tier 3**
> *glottis, photosynthesis, rhomboid, saccule, sambe, conflagration, aileron, vector, irksome*

❋ Here's an example of a core word meaning that is described via the three tiers:

Tier	Vocabulary	Comments
1	*old*	General term for something/someone that is not young
2	*aged, mature, elderly*	More specific vocabulary related to things/people that are "old," but still leaves room for personal interpretation
3	*antediluvian, decrepit, hoary, senescent*	Vivid and specific vocabulary—paints a strong mental picture

The boundaries between the tiers can be a bit fuzzy at times as word knowledge is acquired differently by different individuals. For example, asphalt might be considered a Tier 2 word for a child who grows up in an urban environment; however, this may be a Tier 3 word for a country kid who has never seen a paved road. Consequently, it's important to think about what a student brings to the learning environment when targeting specific words in direct learning.

Vocabulary Sets

Although we often divide vocabulary into oral and written categories, in actuality, we all have four different sets of vocabulary available for communication. These are:

❋ **Listening Vocabulary**

❋ **Speaking Vocabulary**

❋ **Reading Vocabulary**

❋ **Writing Vocabulary**

The most comprehensive set—and the first to develop—is *listening vocabulary* which is comprised of the words we understand. This is the foundation vocabulary upon which the other three sets are based (Think Language/Literacy Hierarchy—see Chapter 1). The next is *speaking vocabulary*—the words we can say and use in conversation. Both are part of our oral vocabulary. The remaining two sets, *reading vocabulary* and *writing vocabulary*, are the written language versions of oral vocabulary. These are the words we understand when we read and those we use in our writing.

Vocabulary

Although dependent on one another, each vocabulary set is used for a different purpose and *all* are necessary in order for a student to be successful in the academic setting. Note the examples of words from different vocabulary sets that are provided in the sidebar. Those who are proficient in oral and written language are able to pass words back and forth among the vocabularies with ease as the situation dictates.

WHAT DOES IT MEAN TO "KNOW" A WORD?

Regardless of the vocabulary set, word knowledge is not an "all or nothing" phenomena. To maximize vocabulary development, students need to learn words in a variety of ways. For instance, vocabulary development does not just involve learning the meaning of a word. Rather, vocabulary development progresses both horizontally and vertically as children learn richer, more complete word meanings as well as multiple definitions for a single word.

> **Vocabulary Sets**
> • • • • • • • • • • • • • • • •
>
> Some words are more easily read (decoded) than said:
> - spasmophonia
> - unwittingly
>
> Some words are more easily spoken than written:
> - through
> - bureau
>
> Some words typically belong only to the spoken vocabulary set:
> - kapish?
> - go figure
>
> Some words are written differently than they are typically spoken
> - clothes
> - Wednesday

For instance, youngsters may use the term *uncle* in their conversational speech long before they have developed the full understanding of the word. A child may initially fast map the word "uncle" as referring to any man. Horizontal development of the word continues as the child begins to understand that an "uncle" is a man who is related to your family, but is not a member of your immediate family. Eventually, he or she figures out that an uncle is a brother of your mother or father. Understanding that the word *bank* can mean a place to invest your money, the area along a river, a mound of snow, or a specific type of basketball shot is an example of vertical vocabulary development.

Vertical and horizontal vocabulary development are key components of becoming word conscious, but there are more! The table on the following page, adapted from the *Put Reading First* Report, provides a useful summary of the different way words can be learned to facilitate the development of a strong vocabulary base. (See next section on Vocabulary Instruction for more principles for effective vocabulary instruction.)

Building Better Readers

Types of Word Learning	Examples
New meaning for a known word	The student has the word in her or his oral or reading vocabulary, but learns a new meaning for the word. *Example:* The student understands the concept of a tree branch. Increase vocabulary by adding branches of rivers and branches of government.
New word representing a known concept	The student is familiar with the concept, but does not know the particular word for the concept. *Example:* The student has a lot of experience with baseballs and globes, but does not understand that they are an example of spheres.
New word representing an unknown concept	The student is not familiar with either the concept or the word that represents the concept. *Example:* The student may be not familiar with either the process or the word photosynthesis.
Clarification and/or enrichment of the meaning of a known word	The student is learning finer, more subtle distinctions or connotations in the meaning and usage of the word. *Example:* The student learns the difference between running, jogging, dashing, and sprinting.

From Put Reading First (NICHD, 2000)

Vocabulary

CHILDREN WITH VOCABULARY DEFICITS

A reduced or constrained vocabulary is one of the hallmarks of children with language delays or language literacy disorders. This is a serious obstacle to the development of reading and writing—which is, of course, critical to success in academic, social, and vocational settings. Lacking adequate vocabulary, and strategies to learn new words, students simply do not have the building blocks they need to effectively comprehend what they read. Furthermore, children with small vocabularies in the early grades learn words at a slower pace than their peers, setting in motion a spiral of negative effects such as frustration, antipathy, and failure, that is difficult to break.

For instance, rather than learning 3000 new root words a year, these students may only learn 1200, causing them to fall farther and farther behind. This suggests that they will graduate—if they graduate—with a vocabulary smaller by nearly 22,000 words than their typically developing peers!

There are a number of reasons why students may not learn vocabulary at a pace that would allow them to succeed in academic and social settings. However, most often, students with special needs do not learn words because of some combination of the following traits:

- **They don't engage in conversation as often as their peers.**
- **They aren't alert to new or interesting words.**
- **They often don't—or don't know how to—listen carefully when they are read to.**
- **They don't read on their own.**

Fortunately, deficits in vocabulary can be remediated with quality instruction. Although vocabulary development is an appropriate and beneficial target for all students, it is especially critical that students who are at-risk vocabulary learners (this includes diverse learners) receive intervention that is both purposeful and empirically-proven to enhance the development of word knowledge and to help them become independent word learners.

Vocabulary can be learned via indirect or direct instruction. Both serve an important, albeit different, role in word learning. However, regardless of the type of learning, vocabulary knowledge is enhanced when words are learned in a natural context and integrated into the student's knowledge base via repetition and connections to the student's life experiences.

Building Better Readers

STRATEGIES FOR BUILDING
VOCABULARY

Building Better Readers

Vocabulary

INDIRECT VOCABULARY DEVELOPMENT

As mentioned previously, typically developing children learn about 3000 new words each year while in school. To achieve this, students must learn approximately *8 new words every single day of the year*. However, research suggests that school-aged students are taught an average of 8-10 words *each week* which translates into about 400 new vocabulary words a year. Applying some simple math reveals a gap of around 2600 words each year that students must learn by some other means each year.

So how do students acquire so many new words? An extensive body of research indicates that the answer is through *incidental or indirect learning*—that is, by interacting in conversations with adults and peers and by encountering new words in text, either through their own reading or by being read to by an adult or more capable peer.

However, this does not mean that we cannot facilitate vocabulary development via indirect learning. In fact, we can do much in the early years to ensure rapid vocabulary development and greater comprehension of grade-level texts in the upper grades. Time and time again, evidence has shown that early intervention through indirect teaching of vocabulary to be highly effective in facilitating vocabulary growth.

Building Better Readers

TALKING/ENGAGING IN ORAL CONVERSATIONS

The more oral language a child has, the more word meanings they learn. For example, Weizman and Snow (2001) found that the quality of the language that young children hear and that of their oral interactions with others is a strong predictor of vocabulary knowledge in later years. This is nothing new to SLPs who are typically masters at engaging children in conversations that are rich in content and appropriate to the developmental level of each individual child. Consequently, we can do much to support vocabulary development by helping parents learn to engage students in rich, interactive conversations in their home environments.

The quality of the oral language experiences at school is also important to facilitating the development of a broad and deep vocabulary. Typically, university training programs for classroom teachers do not include instruction related to oral language development and effective classroom talk. It's not surprising, then, that research has found that classroom language is heavy on closed-ended questions and revolves around topics of "here and now." Further, vocabulary tends to consist of a small corpus of Tier 1 and a smattering of Tier 2 vocabulary words.

> **Recommended resources for facilitating oral language and vocabulary development:**
>
> ✱ It Takes Two to Talk®
>
> ✱ Learning Language and Loving It™
>
> ✱ ABC and Beyond™
>
> **Available from the Hanen Centre**

So, we can encourage teachers to use more Tier 2 words and open-ended questions by modeling good "teacher talk" during collaborative classroom lessons, or by providing in-services or handouts, or even recommending a good resource book or article.

I am a fan of the materials developed by the Hanen Center (see sidebar for examples) and have often recommended—or even provided—these products as a means of creating better oral language experiences and environments. Hanen products are grounded in solid research and are extensively field-tested with parents, teachers, and kids. Highly recommended for facilitating the development of strong oral language skills. Additional titles are listed in the *Resources* section of this chapter.

Vocabulary

READING ALOUD

As important as oral language experiences are to vocabulary development, talking and listening in everyday language is not sufficient to facilitate the kind of vocabulary growth necessary to support strong literacy skills. This is because everyday conversations tend to tap into a relatively small group of vocabulary words that lack the richness and variety that we encounter in written language (books!).

In fact, a study by Hayes and Ahrens in 1988 revealed that children's books contain approximately twice as many infrequently used or rare words than even conversations among college graduates.

For instance, the sidebar provides a sampling of words found in Click Clack Moo: Cows that Type by Doreen Cronin. What terrific words to help children become more word conscious! Although this book has been tagged on Amazon for ages 3-8, the vocabulary listed here is not representative of how we might typically speak to a child of that age.

> *Click, Clack, Moo*
> ● ● ● ● ● ● ● ● ● ● ● ● ● ●
> *exasperated*
> *mediation*
> *concessions*
> *bovine*
> *furious*
> *demands*
> *sincerely*
> *emergency*
> *impatient*
> *snoop*

Exposure to rich vocabulary such as this *in context* is an important building block to helping children develop the kind of vocabulary necessary for comprehension and expression of written language. (Note that I didn't even include the word *typewriter* which may also require a bit of a history lesson!)

So, reading to children—no matter what age or grade—is an important and effective method of building vocabulary indirectly. Children learn new words by hearing them used in context and, when we pair this with conversations about new vocabulary and concepts, we help students link new words to their prior knowledge and experience.

Building Better Readers

While simply reading aloud helps build vocabulary, engaging children in the reading experience through the use of interactive strategies has been found to be even more beneficial in learning vocabulary. Interactive reading, in which the child is encouraged to be an active participant in the reading interaction, helps children learn more new words—and learn them more quickly—compared to reading experiences in which the child is merely a passive listener.

There are a variety of ways to engage children in the reading process, but my go-to strategies are echo reading, paired reading, questioning, predicting, wordless books, and reader's theatre. Working in conjunction with master reading specialist, Helen Davig, I developed the Read With Me!™ program that targets the development of language and literacy skills for pre-school children and their families. However, you do not need to use this program to use interactive reading strategies—you just need to be committed to engaging children as active partners in the reading process!

Echo Reading
Paired Reading
Questioning
Prediction
Wordless Books
Reader's Theatre

❋ To find out more about interactive reading, including how to train parents to use these strategies at home, refer **to Read with Me! Stress-Free Strategies for Building Language and Literacy Skills for Young Children** (Available through Dynamic Resources).

Vocabulary

INDEPENDENT READING

It is also important to encourage students to read on their own. We don't need to focus on "appropriate" reading levels. Rather, we encourage students to read all types of books—some simply for enjoyment and some that may challenge them a bit.

If students only read books that are too easy for them, they won't have the opportunity to learn new words. On the other hand, if books are too challenging, with the majority of words being unfamiliar, the student will not be able to use context to deduce the meanings of unknown words (and may discourage them from reading altogether). The important thing is to get noses into books!

I came across this bit of information while doing some research related to reading and vocabulary development that I thought was compelling. See if you agree.

•••••••••••••••••

If a student reads one hour a day, five days a week, she will be exposed to approximately 2,250,000 words during the school year (yes, that is **TWO MILLION, TWO HUNDRED, AND FIFTY THOUSAND** words!)

•••••••••••••••••

Further if we assume that 2-5% of these words are unfamiliar, she will have encountered 45,000 to 112,500 new words during the year.

•••••••••••••••••

Since research tells us that 5-10% of unknown words can be learned from a single reading, this student will have learned a MINIMUM of 2,250 words in a single year - *simply from reading!*

~Stahl, 1999

USING BOOKS TO SUPPORT VOCABULARY DEVELOPMENT

Studies suggest that 25-50% of vocabulary learning occurs through reading. Consequently, it only makes sense to use books to teach vocabulary in context while simultaneously encouraging a love of reading.

Personally, I look for books that:

* Include rich vocabulary and encourage word consciousness.

* Are rich in context cues to support comprehension.

* Support cognitive organization by presenting words by category or theme.

* Address vocabulary anomalies such as homophones (double meaning words) and homonyms (words that have different meanings but are spelled the same).

* Promote an interest in a particular topic or revolve around a topic about which the child already has an interest.

Here are some of my favorite books for building vocabulary (you can find more in the *Resources* section of this chapter).

What Do You Do? (William Wegman)

Here, each page or two-page spread places one of Wegman's "famous" Weimaraner dogs in a specific vocational setting surrounded by some of the "tools" of that particular trade. Of course, the fun part is that the dog is dressed up to represent the human we might expect to find in that setting.

As we peruse the book, I encourage students to first name the items in the picture (for instance, the mechanic is pictured amid belts, wrenches, oil cans, and so on) and then brainstorm other items that would be appropriate for the job or setting. This creates a natural semantic web—which you may want to map out for, and with, your students. You may also choose to have students write back-stories about the picture/vocation or use the words in some of the other activities that are included in this chapter (and others).

Vocabulary

I Can Do That! (Dr. Suzy Lederer)

Created for very early vocabulary learners, this great little book targets first verbs and gestures. Created by Dr. Suzy Lederer, well-known for her research in early vocabulary, *I Can Do That* provides multiple opportunities for children to hear, see, say, and sign early verbs. With built-in interactive reading strategies, strong rhythm and rhyme patterns, print awareness, and engaging illustrations, *ICDT* provides a multi-modal reading experience that children will want to read again and again.

Imagine (Allison Lester)

Imagine if we were deep in the jungle
where butterflies drift and jaguars prowl
where parakeets squawk and wild monkeys howl....

So begins the first adventure of a group of children who really know how to play! When readers turn the page, they are transported into whatever exotic location the children have imagined. This may be deep in the jungle or down in the depths of the ocean, or even atop the polar icecap. Each double-page scene is filled (actually crammed) with the creatures and other things that one might find in each locale. The border around each spread contains the names of the animals pictured, providing rich vocabulary within a context and encouraging children to search and find each one. Keys to each scene are included in the final pages to help readers who might need a little help identifying previously unknown creatures. Even adults may need to sneak a peek to find the wrasse, or the tiger quail, or perhaps the cock-of-the-rock!

❖ **You may also wish to check out *The Magic Beach* by the same author.**

Capering Cows (Shari Robertson)

When you love building literacy and vocabulary—AND you have a soft spot in your heart for animals doing silly things, you write your OWN children's books. Capering Cows captures the adventures of a sleepless youngster that will keep children entertained and engaged while they learn rich, new vocabulary. Bare cows, hairy cows, friendly cows, and scary cows frolic with cows that slurp, cows that kick, and cows that pirouette and kick.

Capering Cows has been a big hit with children, parents, teachers, and my fellow SLPs. It comes complete with a set of flashcards that can be used to practice the vocabulary and extend the story (and they store in a handy pocket in the back of the book). I recently received a WONDERFUL set of new cow "pairs," artfully illustrated by the imaginative students from Mrs. Darcy Davis-Beghein's class in Goodyear, AZ. Thanks everyone!

❖ **If you like Capering Cows, you may wish to check out the sequel: Shivering Sheep!**

Building Better Readers

Words are Categorical (Brian Cleary)

This is an entire series of books that explore vocabulary by lexical category—verbs, adjectives, adverbs, conjunctions, etc. Examples include *Nearly, Dearly, and Insincerely* (adverbs), *A Mink, a Fink, and a Skating Rink* (nouns), and *To Root, To Toot, To Parachute* (verbs). These books are written at just the right level for upper elementary and middle school kids and include zany pictures and great rhyme.

I also recommend that you check out Brian Cleary's website (www.briancleary.com). It is jam packed with interactive activities and teacher tools for vocabulary development centered around semantic categories.

Language Adventures (Rick Walton)

This series introduces new vocabulary as well as concepts related to morphology, syntax, and language arts in very creative and kid-friendly ways. Lead your students on some Language Adventures with titles such as *Pig, Pigger, Piggest* (Adventures in Comparing) and *Once there was a Bull....Frog* (Adventures in Compound Words). Again, this works particularly well for students who are a bit older. I have used them very successfully with upper elementary and middle-schoolers.

Green (Laura Vaccaro Seeger)

This fun book explores green in all its variations—forest green, sea green, lime green, faded green—each richly illustrated to portray the targeted type of green. In addition, there are some not-so-expected descriptors such as "never green" (a stop sign) and "wacky green" (a green-striped zebra). Visual learners will love this book that also includes cutouts for an enticing peek and a clue about the variation of green that will be explored on the following page.

Eight Ate (Marvin Terban)

Another strategy for building vocabulary is to explore vocabulary anomalies such as homophones (double meaning words) and homonyms (words that have different meanings but are spelled the same). This is a great resource—one I have used for a wide range of ages. It is chock-full of riddles involving word anomalies. Here are some examples:

* "What do you call a large animal with thick fur but no clothes on?"
  - A bare bear
* "What do you call anxious temporary shelters?"
  - Tense tents
* "How do you introduce the potatoes to the main course?"
  - Meet meat!"

Vocabulary

WORDS OF THE WEEK

Word study through books is another powerful way to link reading and oral vocabulary development. Authors use awesome words! For example, in conversation, I might say that I will *put* a book on my desk. An author, however, will typically use vocabulary that is more precise such as *slamming, stacking*, or *arranging*. Or, I might comment that Kristy is *walking* out the door. An author can provide a much richer description, such as *stalking, strolling, stomping,* or even *sauntering,* that helps the reader know how Kristy is REALLY feeling!

So, here is a way to take advantage of the vocabulary authors conveniently provide for us in children's literature that is a bit more structured than reading aloud or having students read books independently.

Method

- ❑ Read a book, or a selection from a book, that includes rich vocabulary (adjust based on difficulty and student age/ability levels).
- ❑ Have students write down three words they don't know or would like to learn more about.
- ❑ Class (or small group of individual student) comes to a consensus (vote, discussion, etc.) of which three to target for the week (or more depending on age/ability levels).
- ❑ Once you have selected the words, come up with "student friendly" definitions together—no copying from a dictionary!
- ❑ Students write down definitions.
- ❑ Say them and read them.
- ❑ Take them home and share with your family.
- ❑ Students search for the targeted words in other places (newspaper, magazines, websites, billboards) and bring in examples or note where they were used.
- ❑ Overuse the targeted word in oral and written language activities all week.
- ❑ Encourage the students to do the same and acknowledge when they use them!
- ❑ Choose new words for the next week.
- ❑ Repeat the sequence.
- ❑ Review one month later.

Building Better Readers

Falling for Rapunzel (Leah Wilcox)

whine	sallied (forth)	plea
curly locks	silky tresses	frills
twine	heaved	swine
hammered	enamored	braid
coincidence	squarely	flattened
chap	nimbly	thrilled
hoot	steed	

There's a Pig in Spigot (Richard Wilbur)

trapeze	seldom	hick
neigh	jitter	furiously
sufficient	explanation	indignation
belfry	notion	lofty
steeple	fictitious	pointed
pantry	inevitable	clatter
holler	hideaway	emphatic
obol	bobolink	dog-fight
bugle	awkward	nausea
spigot	sensible	obvious
sufficient	oblige	enormous
atlas	proprietors	phlox
hacking	clever	smithereens
modesty	demure	monarch

Pest Fest (Julia Duranhgo)

fest	pest	swoon
dainty	hovered	whizzed
stunning	malarkey	shrilling
racket	dreadfully	rant
estate	landlubbing	humbugs
amateur	bleak	unique
matador	heckle	knack
pesky	aggravation	persecution
ace	humble	

Vocabulary

The Cow Who Wouldn't Come Down *(Paul Brett Johnson)*		
tizzy	notion	updraft
"knitted her brow"	contrary	sturdy
"you are the limit"	crest	billowed
crackbrained	hobbled	humming
trough	hearty	squarely

Never, Ever Shout in a Zoo *(Karma Wilson)*		
grouchy	grizzly	charge
dreadful	disasterous	clever
conniving	malicious	mschievous
clatter		

Building Better Readers

The case against using only dictionary definitions

When people first learn words, they understand them as descriptions rather than definitions

(Beck, McKeown, & Kucan, 2013)

WORD	DICTIONARY DEFINITION	DESCRIPTION
Illusion	An erroneous perception of reality	Something that looks like one thing but is really something else or is not there at all

• •

When asked to write a sentence using a dictionary

- 63% of student's sentences were judged to be "odd." (Miller and Garcia, 1985)
- 60% of students' responses were considered by teachers to be unacceptable. (McKeown, 1991, 1993)
- Students did not retain or assimilate information effectively.

Vocabulary

VOCABULARY DEVELOPMENT VIA DIRECT INSTRUCTION

A large majority of vocabulary is learned indirectly through talking and reading. However, incidental encounters do not ensure that students will acquire all the words they need to be successful in all settings. Typically, students cannot learn in-depth word meanings and vocabulary nuances that are necessary for understanding a specialized area of instruction (e.g., chemistry) or a specific literature selection (e.g., *Beowulf*) via indirect experiences only. This is especially true for students with language learning deficits or second language learners who most likely will simply fall farther and farther behind their peers without intentional, explicit, and direct vocabulary instruction.

Unfortunately, there is a lot of vocabulary instruction going on out there is not supported by evidence. For example, research shows that rote memorization of words and definitions is one of the least effective instructional methods of teaching new vocabulary, esulting in little long term effect (Kameenui, Dixon, & Carine, 1987: Baker, Simmons, & Kameenui, 1995). Students who are directed to learn new vocabulary by looking up definitions and memorizing them out of context almost never remember these word meanings after the test. Yet, this technique, which has largely been found to be a waste of time for a majority of students with and without learning challenges, is still in use in classrooms across the country.

So, it's important to engage students using strategies and techniques that have been proven to be effective in building vocabulary knowledge. To that end, research regarding effective vocabulary instruction can be synthesized down to six overarching principles **(as summarized in the sidebar)** that guide us as we plan intervention that facilitates vocabulary development.

The following strategies can be used with all ages: some are a bit more appropriate for younger learners and some for older learners. **However, each addresses at least one, but typically several, of the guiding principles provided by the current literature base.** You can adapt the strategies as appropriate based on the needs of your students to build the vocabulary they need to be successful during their school years and beyond. Each is crafted to help students take ownership of their learning and model how exciting it is to "grow your own vocabulary!"

Research-Supported Principles of Effective Direct Vocabulary Instruction

1. Instruction does not rely on looking up definitions

2. Teaching word parts enhances learning

3. Students must represent their knowledge of words in both linguistic and non-linguistic ways

4. Active engagement and linking vocabulary to personal knowledge is essential

5. Playing with words is an effective way to help students become more word conscious

6. Repeated exposure is essential

Building Better Readers

FOUR SQUARE

Four Squares help students move beyond memorization of definitions and cement the meaning of the word into the student's cognitive schema. Four Squares are appropriate for students from second grade through high school. In fact, they are particularly useful for tier three words that can be challenging for older learners.

All you need for this surprisingly powerful strategy is a piece of paper and a writing utensil. You can use the templates provided in the Resources section of this chapter, create your own template, or simply fold the paper into four quarters! There are a variety of four square models to choose from - or you can create your own.

Method

- ❑ Choose which variety of four square to use based on the needs of the students, or the goal of intervention, or even student preference.

- ❑ Fold a blank piece of paper into half, turn, and then fold in half again to form 4 sections —or select the appropriate template from the resources section of this chapter.

- ❑ Write the targeted vocabulary word in the center of the square, or as indicated.

- ❑ Fill in the quadrants to gain a more thorough understanding of the targeted word.

Here is an example of a Four Square model   (Four Square #1 in Resources section)

Center: Word

First quadrant: *Student Friendly Definition* (this can be from the dictionary, generated by the class or provided by teacher/slp)

Second quadrant: *Semantic Classification* (Noun, Verb, Adjective, Adverb, etc.)

Third quadrant: *Antonym(s) for the original word*

Fourth quadrant: *Synonym(s) for the original word*

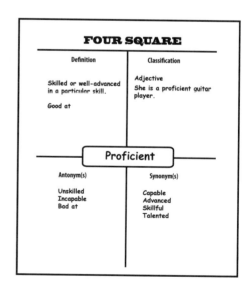

Vocabulary

MORE FOUR SQUARES

There are several different models of four squares.

The Frayer Model (Four Square #2 in the Resources section) uses the same basic framework, but stipulates characteristics, exemplars, and non-exemplars for the quadrants.

Want to try your hand at a Frayer Four Square? Okay! Your word is *"swivet."* Go!

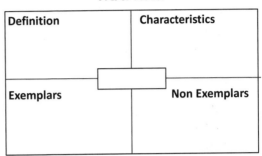

• •

The VVWA Model (which stands for Verbal and Visual Word Association) adds both a visual component and a personal association to the student's understanding of a word. It's a powerful method of really getting students to think about and connect with the targeted word.

Here's an example with the word *"cell."* Four Square #3 template in the resources section is a VVWA model.

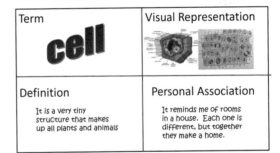

• •

Feel free to get creative!
• • • • • • • • • • • • •
Here is a Four Square for math!

Four Square for MATH!

Definition	Formulas
A parallelogram with four equal sides (Looks like a diamond)	Area formula: $A = b \times h$ (base X height) Perimeter formula: $b+b+b+b$

Rhombus

Visual Representation	Application /Sample
obtuse acute / acute obtuse — Has opposite and equal acute angles and opposite and equal obtuse angles	Find Perimeter 6.7+6.7+6.7+6.7 = 26.8 Find Area: 6.0 X 6.7 = 40.2

PICK SIX

Based on the same principle as Four Square, Pick Six goes a step—well, actually several steps—farther by add two additional boxes to the Four Square model. Pick Six is especially well-suited for use with words that students encounter in academic texts, but may be used for words gleaned from other reading material as well.

For this strategy, students must quote the word as it is used in the original context and then create an original sentence as well as a visual representation. Listing synonyms and antonyms and other forms of the word help firmly establish the new knowledge into the student's working vocabulary.

Here is an example of a completed Pick Six.

Pick Six

Synonyms	Word	Other Forms of the Word
DEAD, NON-LIVING	EXTINCT	EXTINCTION EXTINGUISHED EXTINGUISHER
Antonyms		
ALIVE, LIVING		
Sentence in Text	Picture	Original Sentence
SCIENTISTS HAVE DISCOVERED A LOT ABOUT EXTINCT ANIMALS BY STUDYING THEIR FOSSILS	DODO BIRD	ENDANGERED ANIMAL SPECIES MAY BECOME EXTINCT IF WE DO NOT WORK TO PROTECT THEM

You can find a blank template in the Resources section of this chapter. However, you may prefer to have students fold a blank piece of paper in half longways and then into thirds to create the six sections.

Vocabulary

CONCEPT MAPS

Here is another activity that provides students with a more complete understanding of new terms. You can create concepts maps with a single student, in small groups, or with an entire classroom. As with most of the activities related to learning new word meanings via direct instruction, this activity is appropriate for students of all ages — from early elementary through high school. The example below was completed by a small group of 4th grade students.

Of course, the complexity of the vocabulary will dictate the number of boxes that would be filled in. You can also modify the terminology for older students if you wish, substituting the term *"Definition"* for *"What is it?,"* *"Characteristics"* for *"What is is like?,"* and *"Exemplars"* for *"What are some examples?"*

> A Concept Map template can be found in the *Resources* section of this chapter (and a color coded version can be downloaded from the Dynamic Resources website)

CONCEPT MAP

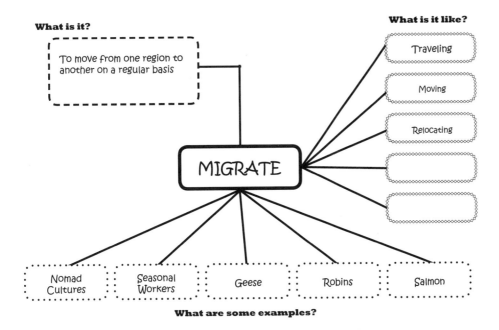

SEEP

(Stem, Examples, Explanations, Picture)

SEEPs help students build both individual word knowledge and general word consciousness through the study of word parts and application of this knowledge to words students encounter in classroom or social discourse. The inclusion of visual representations/pictures to represent the meaning of the word part (which students can draw themselves) creates a powerful word study in one small package.

Here is an example of a SEEP for *"Mal-"*

SEEP

STEM (word part: prefix, root, suffix)	EXAMPLES	EXPLANATIONS	PICTURE
MAL-	MALPRACTICE MALEVOLENT MALODOROUS MALIFICENT (SLEEPING BEAUTY) DRACO MALFOY (HARRY POTTER)	SOMETHING BAD OR EVIL	

This particular example was especially fun as the student had an "ah-ha!" moment regarding one of his favorite movies. "If I had known this before I saw the movie, I would have known that the Malfoy family was bad right from the start!"

As with Four Square and Pick Six, a SEEP template can be created by folding a paper in fourths. However, a template is also provided in the Resources section of this chapter.

> **A SEEP template can be found in the *Resources* section of this chapter**

Vocabulary

BRACE MAPS

This type of graphic organizer assists students in understanding part to whole relationships. Brace maps can be used for any subject or topic; however, I find them particulary useful as a strategy for helping students understand how to break down complex, multi-syllabic words to discern their meaning. Used in this way, Brace Maps provide a visual connection between words and their parts and helps students begin to draw connections to how affixes, prefixes, and word stems work together to communicate meaning.

As demonstrated in the samples below, a multi-syllabic word is placed on the left side of the brace. Each part is then listed on the right side with a brief definition of prefix, suffix, and/or stem. A definition, derived from the combination of the individual meanings, is then created.

Using core vocabulary from a specific unit of study or subject area is an ideal source of words to study. However, in this case, it is also appropriate for the SLP or educator to select words that highlight specific affixes or roots. Alternately, students can identify unknown words encountered in class readings or discussions (or any other setting) that could be evaluated using a brace map to help establish meaning/word knowledge. The key task is teaching students the critical skill of breaking words down into their constituent parts as a strategy for word learning.

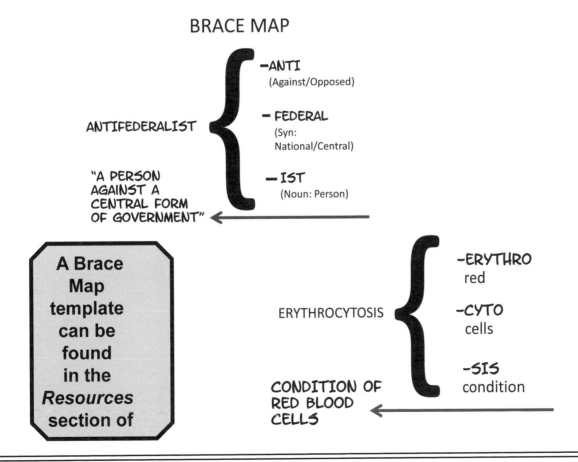

A Brace Map template can be found in the *Resources* section of

Building Better Readers

ALIKE/DIFFERENT

This activity provides practice with compare and contrast fostering both broad and deep vocabulary knowledge. You can have students choose words from a list you generate, or assign words to students, or have students generate the words they want to use. This activity also encourages creative thinking and categorization skills.

Method

❑ Students must think about how words are the same and how they are different and then express these relationships to others.

❑ I use this template. You can have students do this orally or in written form.

> BOTH WORDS _____,
>
> BUT THE FIRST WORD _____,
>
> AND THE OTHER WORD _____.

EXAMPLES

✸ **Targeted Words**: *Skiing, Swimming*

> **BOTH WORDS** are related to sports,
>
> **BUT THE FIRST WORD** is a winter sport,
>
> **AND THE OTHER WORD** is a summer sport.

✸ **Targeted Words**: *Sprinkle, Downpour*

> **BOTH WORDS** describe rain,
>
> **BUT THE FIRST WORD** describes a small amount of rain,
>
> **AND THE OTHER WORD** describes a large amount of rain.

Vocabulary

* ❋ **Targeted Words**: *turtle, elephant*

    BOTH WORDS are animals,

    BUT THE FIRST WORD is a reptile,

    AND THE OTHER WORD is a mammal.

- ❑ This activity can also be implemented using more than two words. Here's a template for 3 words:

    > ALL THESE WORDS _____,
    >
    > BUT THE FIRST WORD _____,
    >
    > AND THE SECOND WORD _____,
    >
    > AND THE LAST WORD _____.

EXAMPLE

* ❋ **Targeted Words**: *elephant, clown, tent*

    ALL THESE WORDS are related to the circus,

    BUT THE FIRST WORD is a circus animal,

    AND THE SECOND WORD is a person in the circus,

    AND THE LAST WORD is an object that is part of the circus.

- ❑ Take time to consider the vocabulary tier as you are selecting words. You can target words from the same tier, or combine tiers. Here are some examples:

EXAMPLE

* ❋ **Targeted Words**: *joy, despair* (Both Tier Two words)

    BOTH WORDS are related to feelings,

    BUT THE FIRST WORD is related to happiness,

    AND THE OTHER WORD is related to sadness.

Building Better Readers

* **Targeted Words**: *Elderly* (Tier Two) *Antediluvian* (Tier Three)

    BOTH WORDS are adjectives related to being old,

    BUT THE FIRST WORD is usually used to describe old people,

    AND THE OTHER WORD is usually used to describe characteristics or old traditions.

* **Targeted Words**: *Photosynthesis, Stoma (*Both Tier Three words)

    BOTH WORDS are associated with plant biology,

    BUT THE FIRST WORD describes the process by which plants convert carbon dioxide to oxygen,

    AND THE OTHER WORD is a part of a plant that allows air and water to enter.

* **Targeted Words**: *Synapse, Nucleus, Dendrite* (Tier Three words related to academic subject student is currently studying)

    ALL THESE WORDS ARE are associated with a neuron,

    BUT THE FIRST WORD describes the space between neurons,

    AND THE SECOND WORD is the center of a neuron,

    AND THE THIRD WORD is a branchy arm at the end of the axon.

Challenge!! It can be fun for students to try to challenge one another to try to come up with ways words are the same and different. (Or, perhaps they would enjoy playing "stump the SLP!") Here are some word pairs my students created when "playing" the same/different "game." I won't share the answers—I'll let you and your students try to figure them out!

House, Vocabulary

Hand, Fathom

Leather, Sunbathers

A pot, A fit

Asphalt, Bread

Vocabulary

WORD SORTS

Word sorts are fabulous activities that can be modified for use with individuals, small groups, or entire classes. The basic premise is to take a group of words and sort them into various categories. The key to making word sorts really work is to encourage students to think creatively about how words can be grouped and labeled. (And then it's time to shuffle them and start over again!) You may need to model the process using self-talk and/or provide quite a bit of scaffolding when students are just beginning to figure out word sorts, but it is worth the time and effort. As students brainstorm, discuss, compromise, and create the categories, they build strong semantic connections and more effectively internalize word meanings.

Method

- ❏ Identify an overarching topic or theme. This might be a subject area or current lesson, a holiday season, sports, or words found in a particular piece of literature or text.

- ❏ Brainstorm words related to the topic and write them on a board.

- ❏ (Optional but recommended.) Have students write the words on index cards. One set of cards for each group.

- ❏ Now comes the fun part. Given the list of words, students begin to sort them into groups of two words or more by some specific parameter. Students then select a label that defines the group.

- ❏ Students continue to sort, group, and label until all words are assigned to a category. Students share their categorization schemes and discuss their rationale for organizing and grouping the words.

See next page for an example of a word sort activity.

WORD SORT EXAMPLE

Word List

design	code	concrete	denouement
draft	devise	conflict	introspective
deduce	concentrate	speculate	enforcement
logarithm	stand	hemispheric	implement
define	continuum	commitment	perspective
area	hypothesize	succinct	complimentary

First Sort

Starts with "d"	Starts with "c"	Starts with "s"	Starts with a vowel	Starts with "h"
design	code	stand	area	hemispheric
draft	concentrate	succinct	introspective	hypothesize
deduce	conflict	speculate	enforcement	
devise	complimentary			
denouement	commitment			
define	continuum			

Second Sort

Multiple Meaning Words	Words that include "ment"	Words that include "spec"	Words with the prefix "de"	Tier 3 words
design	denouement	perspective	devise	succinct
draft	commitment	introspective	deduce	logarithm
stand	enforcement	speculate	define	continuum
conflict	complimentary			hemispheric
concrete	implement			hypothesize
code				

Vocabulary

Variations/Extensions

- Sort random words rather than those associated with a theme.

- Students create a semantic web/map to represent how they sorted and labeled each group.

- Take the same set of words and have students try to sort them into completely DIFFERENT groups.

- Give the words to the student(s) in pre-sorted groups and have the student(s) try to figure out an appropriate label for each.

- Students sort into groups. However, rather than labeling the groups, they challenge another student or group to figure out the sorting scheme(see figure below for an example of a pre-sorted scheme. Can you figure it out?).

- Yes, you can make this competitive! For example, you may wish to time how long it takes for one team to figure out the sorting scheme of the other team and award points for best time per "round." Or award points for each category created by one group or student by another group or student.

- I typically encourage students to add additional words that weren't on the original brainstormed list if they think of something that would fit under a specific label for the chosen theme.

- Bestow fun awards such as "most creative grouping," "largest category," or "best group discussions."

?	?	?	?
devise	continuum	code	area
design	introspective	draft	speculate
deduce	hypothesize	writ	denouement
conflict	hyperbolic		implement
define	hemispheric		perspective
succinct	spectator		commitment
stoic			enforcement

Building Better Readers

DUMP AND CLUMP
(individual Activity)

THE DUMPSTER – All the words related to the topic you are studying (or some other parameter).

THE CLUMPSTER – Pull words out of the dumpster and clump them into categories. Assign labels to each category and write a sentence describing each

This is a variation on word sorts that I use for individual students. Your "dumpster" can be any container that you wish. The activity is essentially the same, but completed with a single students doing the sorting.

Vocabulary

PICTURE IT!

The research tells us that visual imagery strengthens vocabulary so the next set of strategies primarily target representation of new vocabulary through the non-linguistic modes. This is an excellent activity to support vocabulary learning for all students, but especially for those who learn best through the visual channel who will most likely excel here.

I learned about visual learners from my now-adult son who used to illustrate a new term or difficult concept in his notes rather than trying to capture the meaning in words. Although this disconcerted some of his teachers who strongly preferred he take traditional notes, he eventually developed an exceptionally strong oral and written vocabulary—enhanced by his ability to visualize words and concepts in very unique ways. Now, we know that this is, indeed, an excellent strategy for building better vocabulary!

Picture It! can be used to assist in learning a new word OR to deepen vocabulary knowledge of a word for which the student may have some knowledge.

Method

- Have the student write the word somewhere on the page (allow for some artistic expression here. Don't require it be at written at the top of the paper—or any place in particular).

- Then, the student creates an illustration or illustrations (again, in any configuration on the paper that makes sense to them) of any combination of following traits—or others that the student may come up with—that is appropriate for the word:

    - Word meaning (illustrate the word!)

    - General category or topic area from which it is drawn (Science? Literature? Politics?)

    - Location (where might you find this word?)

    - How it's used or how it's done

    - Synonym

    - Antonym

✷ An example of this can be found on the following page.

Building Better Readers

I asked the student to illustrate "ancient" in any way that made sense to him. Once he drew ancient (I'm told this is a monkey temple), he never struggled with the word again.

Vocabulary

IMAGINE A WORD

Here is a variation of using visualization related to vocabulary. This activity is particularly good for visual learners or students who are very artistic. Not only does it help them think more about words in a way that makes sense to them, it gives them a chance to showcase their talent to others.

Method

☐ Students are encouraged to illustrate the meaning of the word by creating art WITH the word. Just like the activity itself, this is easier to show than explain. Here are some examples of what happens when you ask students to "imagine a word!"

Building Better Readers

COMMONYMS (TRI-BONDS)

The research supports playing with words and participating in word games as an effective way to build vocabulary and foster word consciousness.

Commonyms (commercially available as Tri-Bonds) are groups of three words that share a common trait. Here are some examples:

Tree, Car, Elephant	Trunk
Yard, Pogo, Chop	Stick
Softball, Baseball, Vampire	Bat

To figure out the common trait, students must have both broad and deep (horizontal and vertical) knowledge of the words. Solving, and creating, commonyms is an outstanding way to help students build their vocabulary skills and become more word conscious.

Method

- ❑ I suggest that this be played in teams so students can use their collective knowledge of the vocabulary words to solve the problem.

- ❑ Correct answers earn 3 points for the team.

- ❑ Incorrect or no answer opens the door for another team to "steal" for 2 points.

- ❑ If (actually WHEN) individual students blurt out the answer without group input, discuss the importance of building a team consensus and appointing one person to answer the question (this is a great pragmatic lesson!)

❖ You can create your own commonyms, have your students create them, or find them on the websites provided in the *Resources* section.

Vocabulary

Academic Commonyms

Creating Commonyms using academic vocabulary is a powerful way to help middle and high school students delve into word meanings. Creating a commonym requires students to thoroughly understand each of the three words in order to find the common link.

Here are some commonyms created by high school juniors based on academic vocabulary.

Nucleus~Sun~Caramel

Plasma~Money~Gossip

Trachea~Larynx~Epiglottis

Long~Short~Flat

> **See the *Resources* section of this chapter for "Can you solve these Commonyms?" reproducible activity sheets.**

1. center
2. exchanged
3. throat
4. bones

Building Better Readers

HINK-PINKS

Hink-Pinks are word puzzles that result in rhyming pairs. To solve them, students must bring to bear their knowledge of word meanings and fit this into the required rhyming pattern.

➢ Here are some examples:

Move, Female Deer	(Go doe)
24 hours with toys	(Play day)
50% of a giggle	(Half laugh)
A totally cool father	(Rad dad)

Hinkie-Pinkies require an a two-syllable rhyming answer. These are a bit more challenging:

A smelly digit	(Stinky pinkie)
A more elegant knit	(Better sweater)
Loony flower	(Crazy daisy)

➢ **Hinkity-Pinkities** (three-syllable rhyming pairs) are VERY challenging—even for those who have a pretty good vocabulary!

The White House	(President's residence)
A scary pastor	(Sinister minister)

> **See the *Resources* section of this chapter for "Fun with Hink-Pinks" reproducible activity sheets.**

Vocabulary

BUILD YOUR OWN HINK-PINKS!

Creating Hink-Pinks is a higher level vocabulary-building skill than solving them because it requires students to define the word in their own words and think critically about how to connect it with another word. Plus, it's fun to try to stump your friends and teachers.

- First, have students come up with a rhyming pair (silly is just fine!)
- Then, create the definitions for each word.

> Go to *www.squidoo.com/hink-pinks* for a printable worksheet on how to create Hink-Pinks!

ACADEMIC LANGUAGE HINK-PINKS

Hink Pinks can also be created using Academic and Tier Three vocabulary. Try these!

A calm substance that yields hydrogen when dissolved in water

A segment of a circle green space

A 3-dimensional object with equidistant points for an antlered mammal

A small cave slogan.

The students who created these Hink-Pinks with me (11th grade) raved about this activity as a way to help them solidly assimilate academic vocabulary and difficult words into their personal knowledge bases. (In other words, they said they were sure they would never forget these word meanings because they had to really think about how to make them work in a Hink-Pink. Plus, they could always just use each Hink-Pink as a personal mnemonic strategy).

> Go to *www.wuzzlesandpuzzles.com* for lots of great Hink Pinks printable activity sheets!

placid acid
arc park
deer sphere
grotto motto

Robertson

Building Better Readers

WORD LADDERS

Word ladders, sometimes called doublets, are linked to author Lewis Carroll (of *Alice in Wonderland* fame) who supposedly invented them a good long while ago. Word ladders start with two words. Students must solve a series of definition clues to help them move from the word on the bottom of the ladder to the top. The answer to each clue is a word that differs by one letter from the two adjacent words. (Note that the doublets, as originally created by Lewis Carroll, do not include clues.)

Word ladders can be linked to a theme (or not) and can range in difficulty from somewhat challenging to VERY challenging. Word ladders can be any length, depending on the topic and the skill/development level of the students.

Here is an example of a completed 5 step word ladder.

lard	rendered fat
lark	songbird
park	grassy open space in the city
part	piece of a larger whole
cart	two-wheeled conveyance

Find templates for 3, 4, and 5 step word ladders in the *Resources* section of this chapter

Vocabulary

WORD STRINGS/WORD TRAINS

These activities are similar to word ladders in that students create new words using a part of the word that precedes it in. However, these activities require no templates and little prior planning (always a good thing for busy SLPs). Word strings and trains are especially good for facilitating word consciousness, critical thinking, and spelling.

Word Strings

Given a word, students are challenged to create a new word by changing only a single letter. Then, the "new" word is modified again by changing a single letter to create another word. Like this:

word….ward….hard….herd….held…..meld….melt….pelt…..

Word Trains

Given a word, students are challenged to come up with a word that starts with the letter that ends the previous word. Like this:

drink...kind...dinosaur...reason...nice...elephant...taught...tingle……

You can challenge students to create word strings or word trains individually; however, they work especially well in group settings.

Method:

- All players stand.

- Decide if you are going to create word strings or word trains.

- Adult or activity leader writes a word on the board.

- Next person comes up with an appropriate word (depending on whether you are creating word strings or word trains) and writes it on the board next to the first word.

- Each person in line then continues the string/train by building on the word written down by the preceding player.

- Each player must be prepared to define their word if challenged.

- A player who gets "stuck" and cannot create/come up with a new word must sit down.

- Next player can try to add a new word to the string OR can request a new stem to start a new string.

Building Better Readers

Variations/Extensions:

- In competitive play, teams earn a point for each word they add to the string. Last word (when other team is stumped) is worth two points.

- Or, give teams the same starting word and a time limit (your choice). Team with the longest string or train gets two points (or however you wish to score).

- For word strings, you may choose to allow words to be modified by adding or subtracting a letter as well as changing a letter. (e.g., trade/tirade, gate/grate).

- Check out www.briancleary.com for a fun, interactive word train activity.

Vocabulary

DON'T SAY IT! (TABOO)

This activity is based on the commercial game of Taboo in which a player tries to get his/her teammates to guess a word without using specific words. This activity helps students think about vocabulary in new and creative ways.

Method

Step 1 – Prepare the Game Cards

- Select a corpus of vocabulary words with which the students are at least somewhat familiar (such as a current science unit, words from a selection of literature, or current and past "words of the week").

World War II
The Greatest Generation
Hiroshima
Pearl Harbor
Rationing
Veterans

- Students are given an index card on which they are to print a single vocabulary word (typically assigned by you) on the top of the card.

- Next, the student writes five words that describe or are associated with the target word on the lines below.

Step 2 – Play the Game!

- Divide the group into teams.

- For each round, one student on each team is designated as the "giver" and the rest of the students on that team are "guessers."

- Giver from Team A selects (or is given) a card. His/her job is to try to get the guessers on their team to say the word at the top of the card (the targeted word).

- HOWEVER, the words written below the vocabulary word cannot be spoken as they give the clues (i.e., they are "taboo").

- Only members from Team A may guess—but they can guess as often as they want until the word is identified correctly or the allotted amount of time runs out (you decide how long you want this to be).

- A correct guess earns a point for Team A. If time runs out OR the giver says one of the taboo words, no points are earned.

- Game continues in the same manner for Team B (or however many teams you create).

Building Better Readers

Helpful Hints

❖ To insure students do not lose interest, do not allot too much time for each round of guessing.

❖ If students from another team shout out the correct answer, the "active" team may say the word and get the point.

❖ Wikipedia has a complete list of rules and suggestions for a successful game of Taboo. (See *Vocabulary Resources* section for website)

MORE VOCABULARY BUILDING GAMES

JEOPARDY
Create free game boards (no registration required) at:
https://jeopardylabs.com

TWENTY QUESTIONS
Complete directions at:
http://www.wikihow.com/Play-20-Questions

PICTIONARY
Generate Pictionary Words and/or play online at:
http://www.wordgenerator.net/pictionary-word-generator.php

FICTIONARY/DICTIONARY
This is a personal favorite of mine. Find complete directions at:

http://www.ehow.com/how_4443074_play-game-dictionary.html

Vocabulary

SCATTERGORIES

Scattergories is a commercially available game that is a great way to help students build vocabularies and become more tuned into words (word conscious). However, you can easily make your own version.

Method

- ❏ This activity is "played" with a grid.

- ❏ Random letters, both vowels and consonants, are placed in the vertical spaces. (I like to have students pull letters from a "hat" to use in the vertical column.)

- ❏ List categories in horizontal spaces. These can be related to topics being studied in classes (my favorite) or random categories if you are just targeting word consciousness.

- ❏ Students are challenged to find words that fit the categories that start with the designated letters.

- ❏ Encourage students to use all available resources including print, electronic, and social.

Example

	Animals in Africa	Religions of the World	Breakfast Foods	Cities in Europe
M	musk ox	Muslim	milk	Madrid
C	cheetah	Christian	cereal	Canterbury
B	baboon	Baha'i	bagel	Budapest
O	ostrich	Omoto kyo	omelet	Oslow
W	wildebeest	Wiccan	waffle	Warsaw

Building Better Readers

ANALOGIES

Some people may equate analogies to word problems in math. Something you have to learn, but not really useful to "real life." To the contrary! Analogies are an excellent vehicle for vocabulary-building and, by their very nature, facilitate word consciousness. (By the way, word problems really CAN come in handy in "real life" if you happen to be traveling on a train headed west at 60 mph and want to know when you will pass a train traveling east at 45 miles an hour). Analogies are appropriate for supporting vocabulary development of students at virtually any level—from the earliest grades through high school and beyond.

Analogies:Fun
as
SLPs:Awesome!

To complete an analogy, a student must know the meaning of both words and be able to critically compare the characteristics associated with each to make a determination regarding the relationship between the two. Consequently, students are building vocabulary while simultaneously flexing their critical thinking and memory muscles.

The first step in completing an analogy is to identify the relationship between the first pair of words. This, of course, requires a knowledge of the meanings of both these words. Are they synonyms or antonyms? Is there a cause and effect or a part to whole link? Once students figure out how these words "go together," they can much more easily select an appropriate word to complete the second pair. Here are some examples of different types of analogies:

Type of Analogy	Less Difficult	More Difficult
Synonym	big:large::small:little	sweet:saccharin::awful:vile
Antonym	in:out::up:down	inflate:deflate::frail:strong
Part/Whole	wheel:bike::tire:car	paragraph:essay::pixel:photo
Characteristic	cold:snow::sweet:sugar	steamy: tropical::frigid:polar
Cause/Effect	fire:burn::ice:freeze	spin:dizzy::wound:pain
Object/Location	cow:barn::bird:nest	rachet:toolbox::oil:pallette
Classification	purple:color::hammer:tool	mace:weapon::terrier:canine
Action/Object	fly:plane::drive:car	charcoal:sketch::chisel:sculpt
Item/Purpose	fork:eating::crayon:coloring	rasp:smoothing::acid:etching
Product/Worker	smell:nose::sight:eye	portrait:artist::aria:soprano

Teaching analogies can make both students and teachers a bit nervous. Luckily, there is a wealth of material available in printed form as well multiple on-line sources that provide lists of analogies by category, activity sheets, and even entire lesson plans. Several of my go-to sources for analogies are provided in the *Resources* section of this chapter (both in the book lists and web resources sections).

CINQUAINS

How to Build a Cinquain

• • • • • • • • • • • • • • • • •

Line 1:
One word (noun) which names the topic

Line 2:
Two words (adjectives) which describe the topic

Line 3:
Three words (verbs) to express the action of the noun

Line 4:
Four words to express feelings or make an observation

Line 5:
Repeat topic, or one word that sums it up, or a synonym

Based on Japanese haiku, a didactic *cinquain* is a five-line, non-rhyming poem that specifies how particular types of words are used to create a theme (as described in the sidebar). Cinquains can be used to target a number of linguistic skills, but I particularly like them for building vocabulary. They are most appropriate for students over the age of seven.

Cinquains provide students with practice using all four vocabulary sets as they create, edit, and read aloud their poems. Word consciousness is facilitated as students draw from the different vocabulary sets and find ways to use words they know in new ways or find new words to use in familiar contexts.

As an added bonus, reading fluency can be enhanced as students practice reading their poems aloud. Since we will assume the student will read the poem multiple times—we have repeated oral reading practice is built right in! Also, the natural cadence provides practice with prosody without having to worry about coming up with a rhyme.

You can make the task a little more challenging by having students try to write cinquains using only words that start, end, or include a specific sound (great for incorporating into artic/phonology therapy) or link them to classroom curriculum by using vocabulary or themes from current units of study in social studies, science—or anything! The possibilities are endless—I'll leave it up to you to come up with even more creative ways to use this terrific vocabulary-building strategy.

The following page contains sample cinquains that were created "on the spot" during some of my seminars. Note that, despite the simplicity of the structure of the poem, the vocabulary is rich and complex. You can close your eyes and see just what the author is trying to convey.

> **See the *Resources* section of this chapter for a reproducible cinquain template.**

CINQUAINS!

Horses
Beautiful, Gentle
Prancing, Galloping, Dancing
Always make me smile
Friends

Football
Fabulous, Fun
Punting, Passing, Blocking
Cheering for my team
Packers!

Sunset
Colorful, Vivid
Glowing, Spreading, Setting
What a beautiful sight
Masterpiece

Mountains
Massive, Silent
Towering, Growing, Sheltering
Make me feel small
Majestic

Space
Infinite, Mysterious
Expanding, Collapsing, Beckoning
Waiting to be explored
Space

Grandchildren
Precious, Perfect
Laughing, Running, Smiling
Make getting older fun
Grandchildren!

Vocabulary

Here are two examples of cinquains that were developed around a specific academic topic (I call them *super-charged cinquains*). These cinquains were created by a junior and senior - both of whom were identified as language learning delayed.

These were not easy to create. In fact, they required several days of research on the part of the authors. However, the end result was quite extraordinary.

Both students were justifiably proud of their efforts and had developed an exceptionally rich understanding of the academic vocabulary related to the topic and a deeper knowledge of the overarching theme of the cinquain.

Blood
Leukocytes, Plasma
Circulating, Oxygenating, Clotting
Regulates the Body's Temperature
Hemoglobin

LUNG DISEASE
COPD, EMPHYSEMA
GASPING, HEAVING, COUGHING
ALVEOLI DAMAGED FROM SMOKING
PLEURISY

• •

Soil
Terra firma
Nurturing, composting, weathering
More than just dirt
Home

This cinquain was authored by my sister, Merry Kim Meyers, a master teacher of agri-science and a certified landscape architect.

She teaches her students about the difference between the dust under our feet (dirt) and the rich soil that sustains all life. (Merry Kim calls dirt the "D-word.")

I include it here as an example of how cinquains can facilitate vocabulary knowledge, deepen understanding of a topic, and convey deep emotions.

THE MATCH GAME

This activity works well in classrooms or small groups. It promotes active engagement and gets kids up out of their seats and interacting with one another.

Method

- ❏ Choose targeted words. It works best to select half as many words as there are students. (20 students = 10 targeted words).

- ❏ Write each on an index card or something similar (one card per word).

- ❏ Generate definitions as a class.

- ❏ Write the definitions of each of the words from Step 1 on additional cards. (For example, for 10 targeted vocabulary words you would need 20 cards.)

- ❏ Randomly pass cards out to students.

- ❏ Half of the students will receive a card with a word written on it: Half will receive a card with a definition written on it.

- ❏ "Start" the game using any indicator you choose (bell, "Go," lights flicker, etc.).

- ❏ Students try to find their "match." **Warning:** This tends to get a bit noisy!

- ❏ Activity is over when all matches are made.

Extensions/Variations

- ❖ Use a timer to determine how long it takes for all matches to be made. Then shuffle the cards and pass them out again. Class tries to beat their first time!

- ❖ This activity can be played in teams with larger groups.

- ❖ Establish a "no talking" rule so students have to use other means to figure out who has their "match" (such as pantomime).

Vocabulary

SWAT!

Here's another fun, but simple, group or class activity that helps students link words and their meanings.

Method

- ❏ **IMPORTANT!** Start by establishing a *"no swatting anything but the board"* rule. Enforce ruthlessly.
- ❏ Divide students into two teams.
- ❏ List targeted words on the board or post on some other large, flat surface.
- ❏ Give the first player on each team a plastic fly swatter.
- ❏ First members of each team stand with their backs to the word list.
- ❏ SLP or activity leaders provides the definition of the targeted word.
- ❏ First player to turn and SWAT the word that matches the definition earns a point for their team.
- ❏ In the case of a "tie," the owner of the flyswatter on the bottom earns the point for their team.
- ❏ First player hands off the swatter to the next person on their team.
- ❏ REPEAT until everyone has swatted at least once! (Okay to use the same word/definition combo more than once.)

Extensions/Variations:

- ❖ Rather than the definition, the clue could be an antonym, a synonym, a word category, or some other distinguishing linguistic feature of the word.
- ❖ If there is more than one word that meets the requirements of the clue, both players can earn a point for identifying a correct word.
- ❖ Award points liberally and enjoy the energy (and giggles)!

Building Better Readers

UP AND DOWN

This is a quick and easy activity that engages an entire class (or a single student) and keeps them engaged!

Method

- ☐ Give each student a picture or written word (depending on age/developmental level) on a card from a specific vocabulary category.

- ☐ Then, students must stand up or sit down based on whether their assigned word is a part (or not) of a specific sub-category identified by the activity leader.

Example:

Category is **Farm Animals**

> *"Stand up if you live on a farm." (all stand up)*
>
> *"Sit down if you have feathers." (some sit down, continue for each clue)*
>
> *"Sit down if you have four legs."*
>
> *"Stand up if you give milk."*
>
> *"Stand up if we eat your meat."*
>
> *"Sit down if you give us eggs."*

- ☐ When errors occur (e.g., student with "cow" does not stand up under the subcategory "gives us milk"), the SLP/teacher provides feedback at a level appropriate to the student's age/ability.

- ☐ Keep going until you run out of ideas. Then start a new category!

Extensions/Variations:

You can change almost any strategy to meet the unique needs of your students. Here are just a few of my ideas for modifying Monica's basic activity.

- ❖ Students say their vocabulary word aloud each time they stand up or sit down.

- ❖ For older students, you may choose to make this competitive by eliminating students who make errors.

- ❖ In large groups, some students can be "players" (i.e., are assigned a vocabulary word) and some are "judges." The judges monitor the players to determine if they are correct in their decisions to stand up or sit down. Students who do not sit or stand as appropriate are eliminated and become judges. Continue for as long as there are players or you run out of sub-categories or after a specific length of time or whatever other "end" point you choose.

- ❖ Assign a student (or groups of students) a category and have them develop the subcategories for standing and sitting. They then judge or moderate that round of the activity.

Thanks to Monica Gustafson for sharing this great activity!

Building Better Readers

TRIPLE PLAY

This activity can be used with an entire classroom or adapted for smaller groups. You can engage students in a variety of ways. For instance, you may choose to allow one student to give the clues and the rest of the class is allowed to "play" each round without keeping score. Alternately, make it competitive by dividing the groups into teams and keep score. You may also wish to assign some students to special roles such as scorekeeper, team cheerleader, or judge.

Method

- Write targeted vocabulary on index cards (Tier 2 or 3, as appropriate). I suggest aiming for 15-20 vocabulary words for a single large group. Twice as many for two teams.

- There are three "rounds" to this activity. Each targets a different manner of providing clues to guess the word. Students take turns giving the clues to each other, their team, or the entire class.

- To provide multiple opportunities to learn the targeted words, use the same words for each round (so, each word is described via definition, a single word, and pantomime over the course of the activity). However, you could also change this up by using different words for each round or recycling vocabulary from a previous lesson or week to more firmly reinforce the concept.

- For children who struggle with vocabulary, you may choose to allow two students to collaborate to provide the clues or provide some other modification as appropriate.

Round One (Definitions)

Clue-giver draws a card and provides a definition (using his/her own words) for the targeted word. The student can revise the definition as many times as necessary within whatever time limit you provide or until someone guesses the word. Another way to time this is to have each team keep playing until they have guessed all of their words—then have the other team try to beat their time with a second set of words.

Round Two (Single words)

In this round, the student who is giving the clues can only say a single word at a time. This could be a synonym, a rhyming word, or a related word. For example: the targeted word is: "depression." The clue could be "sad" or "1930s" or "dent." This encourages critical thinking and exploration of multiple meanings of the targeted vocabulary word.

Again, only a single word can be used at a time. Someone must make a guess before a new single word cue can be given. Feel free to subtract points for clue-givers who violate the rule!

Round Three (Charades or pantomime)

This round requires the clue-giver to refrain from speaking. Clues must be given only in the form of a pantomime or charade. You may want to first teach students the standard silent cues for charades such as "number of syllables" (hold up appropriate number of fingers) or "sounds like" (cup hand to ear) just to help get the fun started. Guessers can shout out as many guesses as they like, but the clue-giver cannot make any verbalizations. Again, deduct points as you (or your designated student judge) see fit.

Building Better Readers

LAST PERSON STANDING

This is an easy, no-planning activity that requires students to not only think critically about vocabulary, but also to pay attention to what others have said. It can be used in conjunction with a specific classroom lesson or as a stand-alone activity.

Method

- ❏ Everyone in the class stands up.
- ❏ Teacher names a category. For example:
  - Cities in Canada
  - Cartoon characters
  - Names of colors
  - Words to describe a dog
- ❏ First person in line provides an appropriate word to fit the category. Then, the next, the next, and so on.
- ❏ If the student cannot come up with a word with a given time frame (such as 10 seconds), or repeats a word that has already been said, he or she must sit down.
- ❏ Last person standing wins. (No stickers please—pride in a job well done is reward enough.)

Extensions/Variations

- ❖ To keep all students engaged, have students who are sitting down monitor the responses of those left standing to make sure the word fits the category and there are no repeats.

> **Another great activity from the mind of Monica Gustafson!**

VOCABULARY RESOURCES

Vocabulary Resources

BOOKS THAT BUILD VOCABULARY

A is for Angry: An Animal and Adjective Alphabet	Sandra Boynton
Analogies for Beginners	Diane Draze & Lynne Chatham
Beach is to Fun: A Book of Relationships	Pat Brisson
Behind the Mask: A Book about Prepositions	Ruth Heller
Big Blue Whale	Nicola Davies
Biggest, Strongest, Fastest	Steven Jenkins
Capering Cows	Shari Robertson
The Cow Who Wouldn't Come Down	Paul Brett Johnson
Dear Deer: A Book of Homophones	Gene Barretta
Eight Ate: A Feast of Homonym Riddles	Marvin Terban
Falling for Rapunzel	Leah Wilcox
Green	Laura Vaccaro Seeger
Hairy, Scary, Ordinary	Brian Cleary
Herd of Cows! Flock of Sheep!	Rick Walton
Hottest, Coldest, Highest, Deepest	Steven Jenkins
How Much Can a Bare Bear Bear?	Brian Cleary
If You Were a Homonym or a Homophone	Nancy Loewen
If You Were Onomatopoeia	Speed Shaskan
If You Were a Prefix	Aboff

Building Better Readers

I Can Do That!	Suzy Lederer
Imagine	Alison Lester
Jack's Garden	Henry Cole
Kites Sail High: A Book about Verbs	Ruth Heller
Magical Beach	Allison Lester
Mine, All Mine: A Book about Pronouns	Ruth Heller
A Mink, A Fink, and a Skating Rink	Brian Cleary
Miss Alaineus	Debra Frasier
Nearly, Dearly, Insincerely	Brian Cleary
Nouns and Verbs Have a Field Day	Robin Pulver
Once There was a Bull…(Frog)	Rick Walton
Painless Vocabulary Series (particularly good for middle and high school)	Michael Greenberg
Pest Fest	Julia Durango
Shivering Sheep	Shari Robertson
There's an Ant in Anthony	Bernard Most
There's a Pig in the Spigot	Richard Wilbur
Things that are MOST in the World	Judi Barrett
Up, Up, and Away	Ruth Heller
Unlocking Analogies: Grades 4-5	Marianne Tatom
What Do You Do?	William Wegman
Word Wizard	Cathryn Falwell

Vocabulary Resources

WEB-BASED VOCABULARY-BUILDING RESOURCES

www.briancleary.com
- packed with fun interactive vocabulary building activities. Most are centered around semantic categorization

www.freerice.com
- each question answered correctly donates 10 grains of rice to a country in poverty. Words get harder as you get more correct.

www.sheppardsoftware.com/web_games_vocab.htm
- games that help students identify nouns, verbs, adjectives and more

www.enchantedlearning.com/wordladder/
- word ladders

https: jeopardylabs.com
- create your own jeopardy board or use a pre-made board

www.puzzlechoice.com/pc/Wordladder_Mex.html
- more word ladders

www.wuzzlesandpuzzles.com
- lots of vocabulary/word consciousness activities here! Commonyms, hink-pinks, mad gabs, and more

http://wordcentral.com/buzzword
- a new vocabulary word everyday plus other activities

www.madglibs.com
- great for building vocabulary by word category—also great for comprehension monitoring

http://school.discoveryeducation.com/brainboosters/wordplay/hink-pink.html
- more hink-pinks

www.squidoo.com
- hink-pinks, commonyms, and other word building activities

www.vocabulary.co.il/
- provides a wide variety of vocabulary games and activities (including analogies by grade level). A number are specifically for ELL students

http://www.spellingcity.com/analogies.html
- resources, activities, and information related to analogies

http://www.quia.com
- just type "analogy" into the search box and watch what happens! (These activities will keep your students busy and engaged in building vocabulary for weeks!)

http://www.asha.org/Publications/leader/2011/111101/Builidng-Vocabulary-with-Online-Tools.htm
- just as good as it sounds…

TEXT-BASED VOCABULARY-BUILDING RESOURCES

Beck, Isabel L., McKeown, Margaret G., & Kucan, Linda. (2002). Bringing words to life. New York, NY: The Guilford Press

Montgomery, Judy K. (2006). The Bridge of Vocabulary: Evidence-Based Activities for Academic Success. San Antonio: Pearson.

Robertson, S. & Davig, H. Read With Me! Stress-Free Strategies for Building Langauge and Early Literacy Skills. Indiana, PA: Dynamic Resources.

Products Available from Hanen Centre (www.hanen.org)

It Takes Two to Talk®

Learning Language and Loving It™

Let Language Lead the Way™

Encouraging Language Development in Early Childhood Settings™

Fostering Peer Interactions in Early Childhood Settings™

Teacher Talk™

Vocabulary Resources

FOUR SQUARE #1

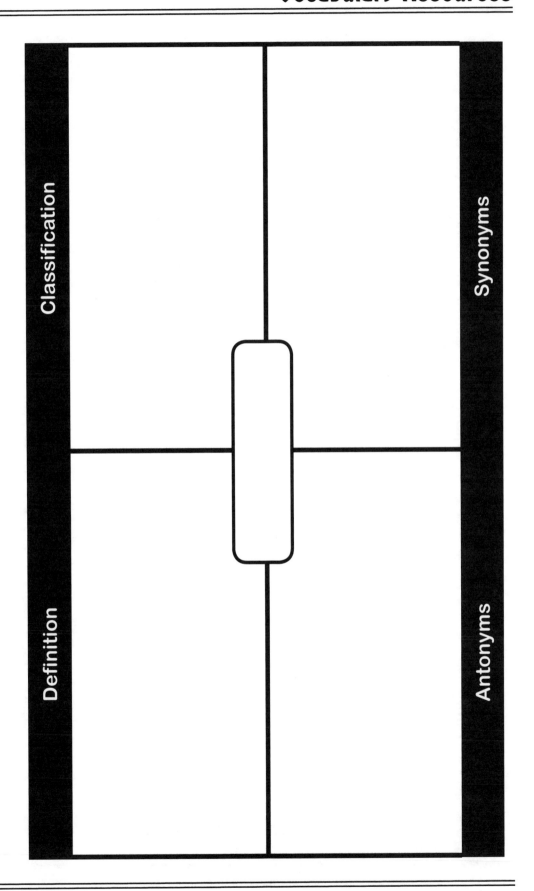

| Classification | Synonyms |
| Definition | Antonyms |

Reproducible for Educational Use- Dynamic Resources

Building Better Readers

FOUR SQUARE #2

Exemplars	Definition
Non-Exemplars	Characteristics

Vocabulary Resources

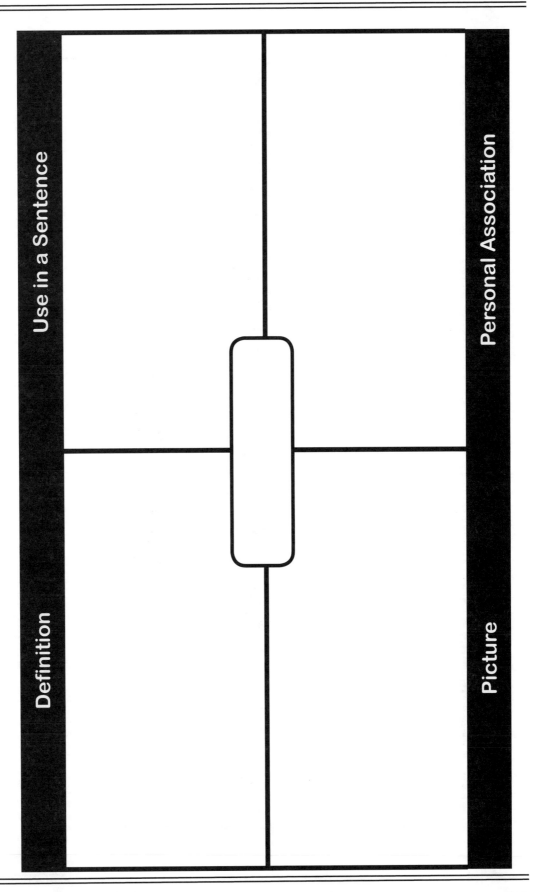

FOUR SQUARE #3

- Use in a Sentence
- Personal Association
- Definition
- Picture

Building Better Readers

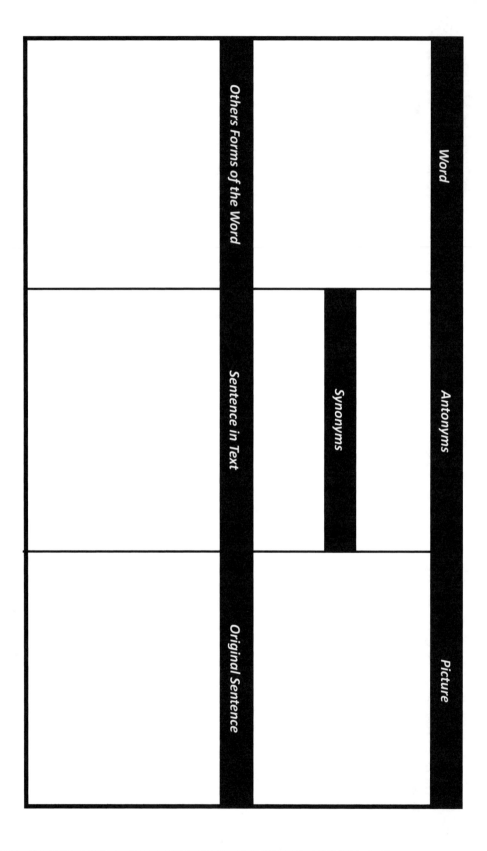

192 Reproducible for Educational Use- Dynamic Resources

Vocabulary Resources

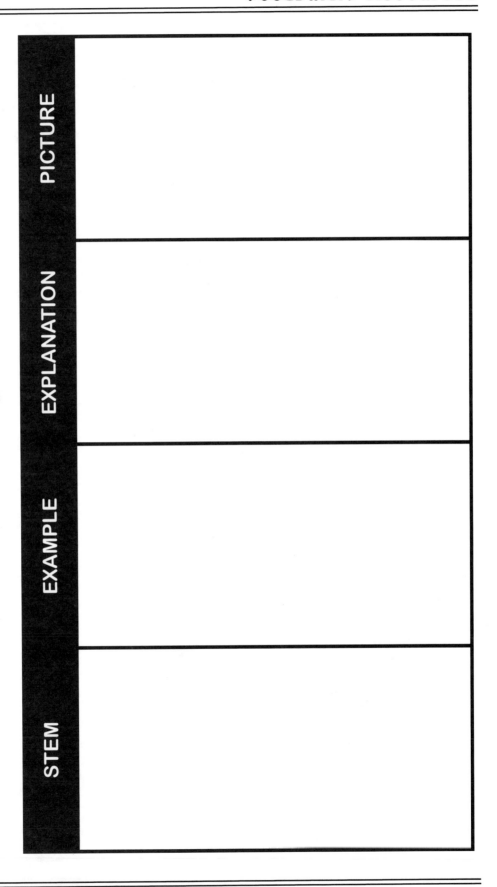

Reproducible for Educational Use- Dynamic Resources 193

Building Better Readers

BRACE MAP

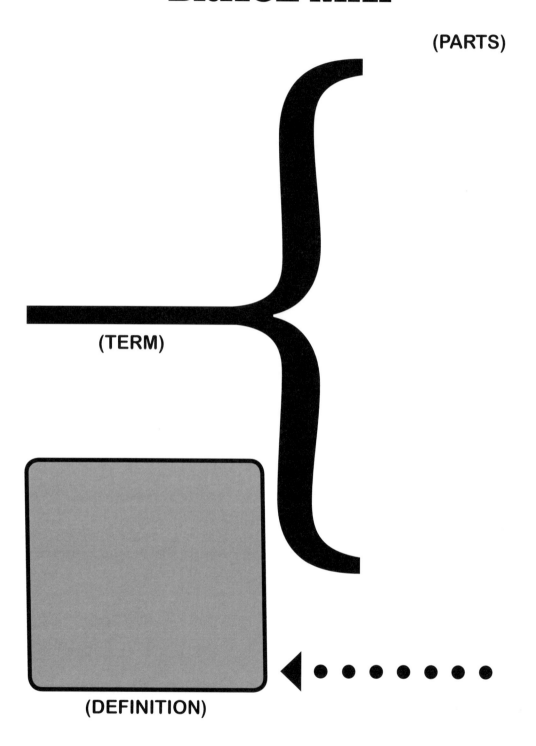

Vocabulary Resources

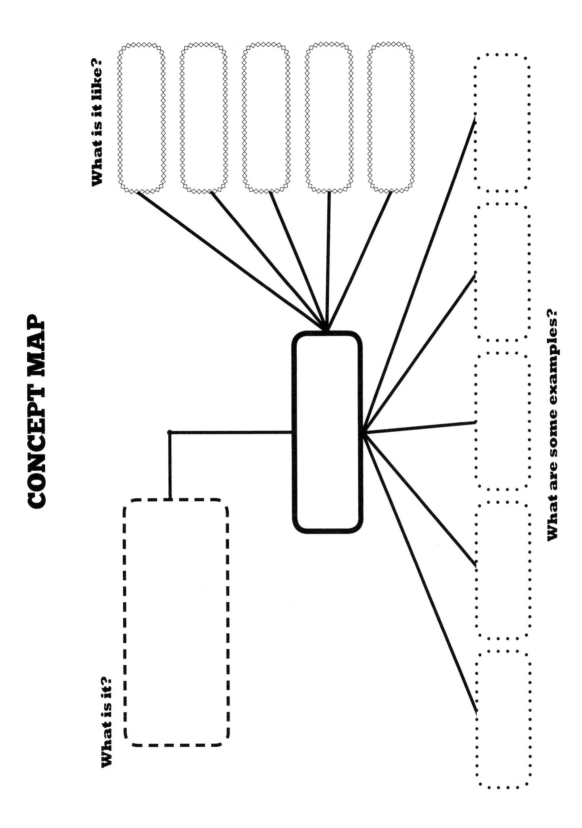

Reproducible for Educational Use- Dynamic Resources

Building Better Readers

CAN YOU SOLVE THESE COMMONYMS?

Ball~Fish~Cold

Cork~Question~Balloon

Bottle~Baseball Player~Mushroom

Bell~Mouth~Shoe

Tug of War~Boat~Nightly News

Fog~Jack~Body Builder

Hockey Game~Restaurant~Bank

Vocabulary Resources

MORE COMMONYMS!

Basketball Court~Highway~Bowling Alley

Punch-Volleyball-Hair

Radio-Car Engine-Piano

Florist~Furniture Store~Obstetrician

Create Your Own Commonyms!

1.
2.
3.
4.
5.

Building Better Readers

FUN WITH HINK-PINKS!

A boring choo-choo ....

A cap that was sat upon ....

A cloudy 24 hours ....

Leave, female deer! ....

Rotund kitty ....

Small rodent abode ....

Angry male parent ....

Tardy companion ....

Sandy fruit ....

Pretty female horse ....

Beach orchestra ....

Sparkly finger jewelry ....

Vocabulary Resources

HINK-PINKS AND MORE!

A twisted penny ....

A sun-kissed male ....

A washed legume ....

NOW LET'S TRY SOME HINKIE-PINKIES!

Improved writing ....

Bunny routine ....

Turbulent sauce ....

READY FOR SOME HINKITY-PINKITES?

Believable food ....

Frozen pedal vehicle ....

Evil holy man ....

**Now, make up your OWN Hink-Pinks on the back!
(Try a couple of Hinkie-Pinkies, too!)**

Reproducible for Educational Use- Dynamic Resources

Building Better Readers

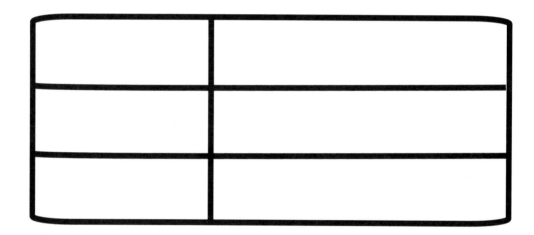

WORD SORTS

Vocabulary Resources

Word sorts are fabulous activities that can be modified for use with individuals, small g

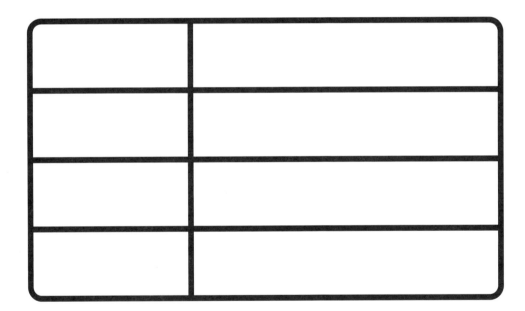

Reproducible for Educational Use- Dynamic Resources

Building Better Readers

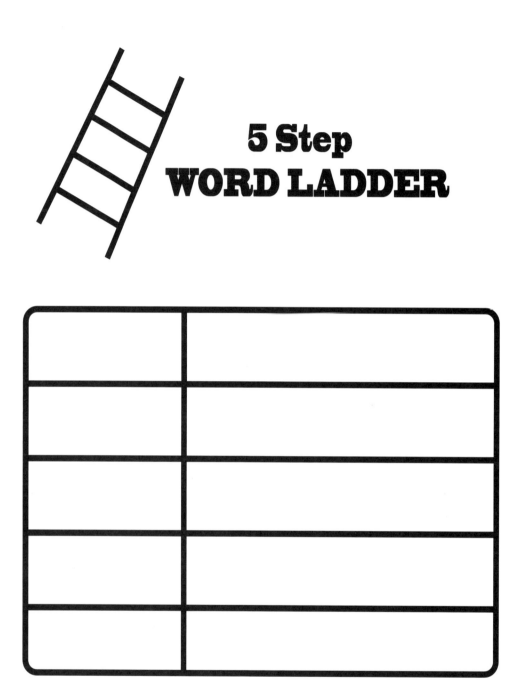

5 Step WORD LADDER

Vocabulary Resources

BUILD - A - CINQUAIN

_____
Noun

_____   _____
Adjectives (describe the noun)

_____   _____   _____
Verbs (describe action of the noun)

_____   _____   _____   _____
Observations or Feelings

_____
Restate Noun or Synonym

ANSWER KEYS

CAN YOU SOLVE THESE COMMONYMS?

*Can be popped

*Have a tongue

*Lift

*Can be caught

*Have caps

*Have an anchor

*Have checks

MORE COMMONYMS!

*Have lanes

*Can be tuned

*Can be spiked

*Make deliveries!

FUN WITH HINK-PINKS!
- Plain train
- Flat hat
- Grey day
- Go, doe
- Fat cat
- Mouse house
- Mad dad
- Late date
- Beach peach
- Fair mare
- Sand band
- Bling ring

HINK-PINKS AND MORE!
- Bent cent
- Tan man
- Clean bean

- Better letter
- Rabbit habit
- Wavy gravy

- Credible edible
- Icicle bicycle
- Sinister minister

CHAPTER 6

Comprehension

The final task of independent reading is **text comprehension**—the whole reason for reading! Text comprehension is a complex skill that is difficult, if not impossible, to isolate and target as an individual entity. On the one hand, we know that phonemic awareness, knowledge of phonics, appropriate levels of reading fluency, and a robust vocabulary all contribute to reading comprehension. As such, children who lack these skills will likely struggle when trying to extract meaning from written language.

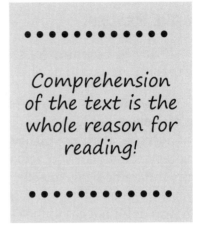

Comprehension of the text is the whole reason for reading!

On the other hand, we cannot assume that comprehension occurs merely because these prerequisites for reading are in place. So, while we know these skills are absolutely necessary, they may not be sufficient for comprehension to occur. In short, comprehension is more than just the sum of its parts.

However, we do know that good readers have in common two key core characteristics above and beyond the four skill areas targeted in previous chapters. Specifically, good readers have a **purpose** for reading and they are **active** in the reading process. Both of these characteristics substantially affect a reader's ultimate comprehension of the material. Consequently, we can facilitate text comprehension by encouraging our students to become active, purposeful readers.

READING WITH A PURPOSE

Consider how the concept of having a purpose affects us in our daily life. When you get up in the morning, you may take a shower, choose what you will wear, eat breakfast, feed your pets, and any number of other tasks. Regardless of the list, you have a purpose for getting up and getting moving! Perhaps your purpose is to get to work on time, or to meet a friend for coffee, or get to your dentist appointment, or even to catch a plane to start your vacation (that's my favorite one). But, you set your alarm and complete these tasks because you have a **purpose**. Similarly, you do the laundry, dust, wash dishes, or vacuum because you want your house to be a pleasant place to live – another purpose. (Alternately, it could be because your mother-in-law is coming to visit and you don't want her to know how you *really* live...but that's a purpose too!) Your purpose might not always be pleasant or fun (case in point, dentist's appointment), but you are aware of it and you shape your behaviors to accomplish it.

But what happens if you haven't identified a purpose? You most likely end up dawdling around, aimlessly puttering at this and that, getting nothing accomplished and before you know it, your day is over—and you probably have no idea where it went! (Okay, sometimes this is good for us, but bear with me!)

The same principle applies to reading. When you pick up written material, you typically have a reason for reading it. Purposes for reading may include gaining information about a

Building Better Readers

particular topic of interest to you, reading a travel guide to prepare for an upcoming vacation, completing an assignment, keeping up with current events via the newspaper or web, or even just reading for the pure enjoyment of getting lost in a story. However, if you don't know why you are reading something, the chances are you won't really connect to the text and won't remember what you read—even if you have all the foundation skills of reading in place!

Active Readers

Having a purpose for reading is important, but successful readers must also be *active* in the reading process to be able to comprehend text during independent reading.

For instance, if you are driving across the state to visit a friend (your purpose) but you are not actively engaged in the process of driving, chances are you will not be successful in fulfilling your purpose. Perhaps you have all the skills and prerequisites that are necessary for a successful long distance drive—you actually own a car, you have a driver's license and understand speed limits and traffic signs, you own a GPS, and can read a map when technology fails. However, if you don't engage or utilize those skills and prerequisites—you don't open the map or turn on your GPS, you don't put gas in the car, you don't pay attention to exit signs, you neglect the thumping sound of a tire going flat—you may end up somewhere, but probably not where you planned!

Readers who are active in the reading process use meta-cognitive strategies to *think* about what they are reading. They engage in self-questioning to determine what they already know and what they don't know about the topic of the selected text. They use context clues to derive possible meanings for unknown vocabulary words and strive to make personal connections with the reading material.

Facilitating Reading Comprehension

Typically, students who struggle with reading comprehension do so because they don't know how to engage in the reading interaction. They don't understand the power—or in many cases, even the concept—of active, purposeful reading. We facilitate reading comprehension by attending to the prerequisite skills discussed in the previous chapters and by taking time to explicitly teach student about THEIR role in the reading process.

Strategies for Building
Reading Comprehension

Comprehension

WORDLESS BOOKS

Wordless books are my go-to resource for targeting many different skills related to literacy—including reading comprehension. (They can also be used to facilitate higher level skills such as critical thinking, sequencing, vocabulary development, and perspective-taking). Since the story is told through the illustrations, students become the "author" by creating text to communicate the story as they interpret it. This provides a *purpose* and promotes *active engagement* as students have to create a storyline while simultaneously managing vocabulary selection, writing mechanics, spelling, and grammar.

The basic technique follows a simple four-step process:

1. **Preview the book.**
2. **Student writes the text to tell the story.**
3. **Edit to create a finished product.**
4. **Share with others**.

To expand a bit on this basic sequence, I typically go through the book with the student using open-ended questions and predicting to encourage critical thinking about the story. For an older student, you may prefer to have them preview the story on their own to encourage active engagement. However, this requires a certain level of motivation that may be lacking in struggling readers, so be prepared to step back in and provide some scaffolding as necessary.

I like to use sticky notes when developing the text for the student's version of the story. Depending on their current skill levels, you can have students either write directly on the sticky note or have them dictate the story to you or another adult. The beauty of this technique is that the sticky notes can easily be removed if editing is required and replaced with a "fresh" note. I suggest first having the student just get their ideas down, then go back and edit for content and sequencing. Next review and think about the vocabulary—can more descriptive, more precise, or more colorful words be used to make the story sparkle? Is the "tone" of the story right for the targeted audience? This process may occur many times as the student makes changes in the content of the story. Lastly, edit for spelling, grammar, punctuation, and writing mechanics.

> *Using sticky notes to add text to wordless books allows for multiple revisions with minimal fuss.*

Working with wordless books also provides practice with reading fluency (through repeated oral readings) as you will ask the student to read and re-read the text as they make edits until the story is "just right." Eventually, have students share their finished stories with other students, their families, or some other audience.

Building Better Readers

Many people make the incorrect assumption that wordless books (sometimes referred to as merely "picture books") are only for younger children. On the contrary, wordless books can tell quite complex stories using very sophisticated illustrations. In addition, the term *wordless* can be a misnomer. In fact, many wordless books actually have words; however, the words do not tell the story. That is left up to the imagination of the reader!

Here's a selection of my favorite wordless books. I have used them again and again with great success. You'll find even more in the *Comprehension Resources* section of this chapter.

Tuesday (David Weisner)

The first page states, *"Tuesday evening, around eight..."* When the intrepid reader turns the page, he or she is treated to the sight of frogs rising out of the swamp on lily pads. They are soon joined by a whole squadron of aerial amphibians who sail out over the countryside and descend upon a nearby town. From the startled gentleman who notices what he thinks are flying frogs out of the corner of his eye when tip-toeing into the kitchen for a midnight snack, to the old lady who has fallen asleep in front of the TV and is unknowingly joined by a host of froggy friends hovering around the late show, this book is packed with detail and humor. Even after the frogs return to the pond, the reader is left with a hint of what might come *next* Tuesday.

Good Dog Carl (Alexandra Day)

I believe that there are two types of people in this world. Those that think the *Good Dog, Carl* series is hilarious fun and those that think the rest of us are seriously disturbed (probably true). This first book of the series is representative of those that follow. Carl, a big friendly rottweiler (yup), is left in charge of the baby who is sleeping peacefully in the crib, while Mom runs a few errands. Carl makes a quick check out the window to make sure the coast is clear. Then Baby climbs out of the crib and onto Carl's back and the adventures commence! From jumping on the bed to taking a dip in the aquarium, Carl and Baby enjoy a fun-filled afternoon of hijinks that even includes raiding the fridge for a snack. But, savvy Carl keeps one doggy eye on the clock and has everything cleaned up and in order before Mom returns home.

Time to call child protective services or just roll with the punches? I always choose the latter and Carl and I have helped many students learn that it's okay to venture into the realm of "completely silly" while learning to develop storylines.

Comprehension

Good Night Gorilla (Peggy Rathman)

"Good Night, Gorilla," says the zoo keeper on every page, but the Gorilla, who has stolen the zoo-keeper's keys, has other plans. One by one he lets each of the animals out of their cages. An armadillo, a giraffe, a lion, and a hyena are only a few of the creatures who tip-toe home behind the zoo keeper to snuggle in for the night. My favorite page involves the zookeepers wife —well, actually only her eyes—as she realizes that her bedroom has been transformed into a den in every sense of the word.

Flotsam (David Weisner)

With a title that is in itself a mini-vocabulary lesson, Flotsam is another winner of a wordless book from David Weisner. When an inquisitive young beachcomber finds a barnacle-encrusted camera washed up on the shore, he begins a fascinating journey of fantasy and "what-ifs?" The developed film reveals mechanical fish swimming with the more traditional fin and gill variety, tiny aliens vacationing with some weirded-out seahorses, and whole civilizations living on the back of a starfish. But the story doesn't end there. When he gets out his magnifying glass, the young explorer discovers there is more to the pictures than what first meets the eye.

Who says a book needs words to target a wealth of rich vocabulary? You can "mine" this treasure for weeks and expand the lesson in as many directions as your imagination—or that of your students —can take you.

The Polar Bear Waltz (Outside Magazine)

This book is made up of photographs collected by the editors of *Outside Magazine* that portray funny, oddball, or amazing moments related to animals and/or the outdoors. There are no words on the page other than the name of the photographer who took the photo and where it was taken. Some favorites include a flock of sheep surrounding a sign that says "soft shoulders," a squawking bird perched on a loud speaker, and the frozen, stiff result of long hair, a hot spring, and freezing temperatures. Some of the pictures are the result of true serendipity (a cloud that looks like a person blowing smoke rings) and some portray kind of a "take that, human!" mentality (e.g., a lion munching on a video camera).

For me, the key to using this book is to allow students to select a photograph that interests them and then asking them to write a "back story" that explains how the picture came to be or to tell the story of the person or animal involved. If you like, you could make it a class project so each of the photos has a story to accompany it.

WHAT'S MY PURPOSE?

It is easy to assume that students intuitively understand the purpose of a reading assignment. For instance, a classroom teacher very likely expects that their students understand that the purpose of reading assigned text is to learn the material well enough to participate in classroom discussion, or answer a series of questions, or apply the material to a class activity or an exam. Although never explicitly stated, many of the students in the class will understand this purpose.

However, a struggling reader's purpose is often to just be able to get through the passage. So, in the mind of this reader, once the assigned text has been read all the way through, the purpose is fulfilled. Unfortunately, this mismatch in expectations is a recipe for disaster. From the teacher's point of view, the student is lazy, doesn't follow directions, or doesn't care. The student is mystified as to why the teacher is upset and may eventually just stop trying altogether.

Consequently, it is important that we explicitly discuss various purposes for reading. Then, we provide students with practice self-identifying the purpose for reading a specific passage.

Method

- Start by having students brainstorm potential purposes for reading. You may have to provide quite a bit of scaffolding for this step. In fact, particularly for younger students, you may have to actually provide a list of purposes as the first step.

- Next, provide students with different reading scenarios and ask them to identify possible potential purposes for reading the text selection.

- To keep intervention functional and linked to classroom curriculum, have students bring their assignment books (or work with teachers to obtain reading assignments) and identify the purpose of assigned readings.

- NOTE: You may need to extend this activity by teaching students how to ask their teacher, or whomever assigned the text, for an explicit explanation of the expected purpose of the reading assignment.

Comprehension

Here's an example of a worksheet you may choose to use to help students identify the purpose of their reading interactions. In many cases, more than one purpose may apply to a single reading selection. I encourage students to clip this checklist to the front of the book, article, or assignment as appropriate to remind them of their "job."

WHAT'S MY PURPOSE?

Text Selection _____
(example: title of book, chapter, article, page range, etc)

- ☐ Read for pleasure
- ☐ Read to learn new vocabulary
- ☐ Read to be able to discuss with others
- ☐ Read to learn a procedure
- ☐ Read to find answers
- ☐ Read for specific information
- ☐ Read to compare and contrast
- ☐ Read and reflect
- ☐ Read and summarize
- ☐ Other _____

A full-sized, reproducible version of this worksheet is available in the Resources section of this chapter.

NAME THAT PURPOSE

It is important for students to identify their purpose for reading. However, just like oral language, written language is a two-way street. It requires both a receiver (the reader) and a sender (the author). So, we can help students improve comprehension of written text by helping them understand that effective authors also must have a purpose for writing. In this way, we help students gain a better understanding of text by teaching them the different ways authors can structure text to convey meaning.

For example, authors may write to:

❑ Tell a story

❑ Compare and contrast

❑ Convince an audience

❑ Convey information

❑ Entertain

❑ Report and inform

❑ Share an experience

> A reproducible worksheet combining reader and author purposes can be found in the *Comprehension Resources* section of this chapter.

Comprehension

HERE'S WHAT I THINK

This strategy doesn't involve teams, templates, or pre-planning. It isn't fancy or particularly creative. However, it *is* an extremely powerful way to provide a live demonstration of how an effective reader engages with text. I like to think of it as **thinking out loud**. Although simple on the face of it, use of this strategy can result in a big payoff for students who struggle with reading comprehension.

However, there is a caveat. Because this is mostly a "spectator sport" (i.e., students are not as actively engaged as other strategies), it is best done in small doses and with text that has a high level of interest to students.

> *While effective, it is best to use this strategy in small doses and in conjunction with other activities that promote reading comprehension.*

Method

- ❏ Read aloud from a selection of text that is appropriate for the age and ability level of the student/s.

- ❏ Stop reading at suitable intervals to explicitly model active engagement and comprehension monitoring. (You'll find some examples in the chart on the following page.)

- ❏ Engage student/s in the process as appropriate by periodically asking them to suggest thinking strategies or to identify the strategy you are using to help keep them engaged.

> **See next page for some *"Here's What I Think"* self-talk examples.**

Self-Talk Strategies

Strategy	Self-Talk Examples
Prediction	"I'll bet someone is going to eat that apple pie Samantha left on the window sill!"
Questioning	"Is the author trying to mislead me so I draw the wrong conclusion?"
Personal Connection	"This article is about hearing loss. My grandmother was born deaf. According to the information here, she must have had a sensory-neural type of loss."
Decoding	"That's a hard word. I'd better take time to sound it out."
Unknown Word—Using Root Word	"I don't know what rampion is, but since it "grows in a garden" I'll bet it is an edible plant."
Unknown Word—Using Morphemes	"I know that satisfactory means okay and I know that the prefix un- means "not" or "opposite" so unsatisfactory must mean something is not okay."
Unknown Word—Using Context	"I know what physical means, so physicality must have something to do with the shape or characteristics of something."
Summarizing	"This article was about candle making and specifically how to make scented candles."

Comprehension

PREDICT-IT!

We can help students become more purposeful and active in reading by engaging them in tasks that follow a ***predict-read-review*** format as is used in this strategy. This primes the student to listen for specific vocabulary or components of the text, thereby providing a purpose and encouraging active engagement. If you like, you can add a little competitive "carrot" to spice things up (see suggestions below).

This particular activity is extremely flexible. You can use it with individual students or with groups. You can use it with very young children as a completely oral activity (I have used this with preschool groups with great success) or with much older students as a consensus-building and logic activity.

Method

- First, show student/s the cover of the book and, depending on how you want to structure the activity and the age of the participants, perhaps some illustrations as well.

- **IMPORTANT**—don't share or show any words other than the title.

- Next, ask the student/s to predict words that they think the author might have used to tell the story.

- Read the story. For younger students, I prefer to read the story aloud. For older students, you may choose to have them read the story independently either silently or aloud.

- Students keep track of the words they predicted that were used in the text.

Extensions/Variation

- There are a number of variations for this strategy. Obviously, this lends itself to a group activity—large or small.

- If you use this with a large group, you can break the students into smaller groups and have them brainstorm the predicted words.

- A friendly competition to see who predicts the most words correctly can be a lot of fun.

- For an older class, you can ask them to negotiate and come to a consensus on their top ten words—with reasons for their selections.

Building Better Readers

- ❖ I have also asked students to predict words that they think would NOT be in the book—which adds an interesting twist to the activity and is harder than you might think.

- ❖ I have had some excellent discussions stem from this activity as we talk about why some words might not have been included that were predicted and vice versa.

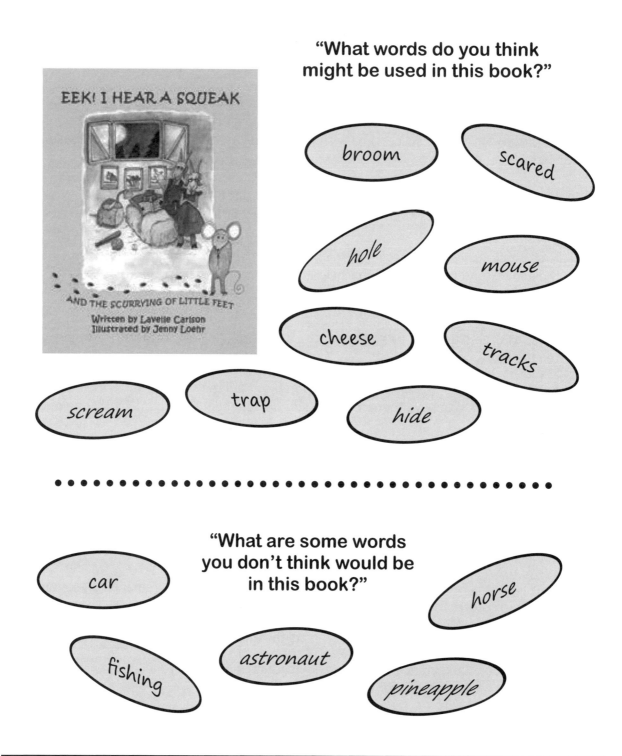

Comprehension

PREDICT-A-STORY

Here is another strategy that utilizes the **predict-read-review** format. To be successful, students must have a working knowledge of the components of story grammar (e.g., setting, characters, problem, action, resolution, etc). Consequently, if students have not been exposed to story grammar, you will need to pre-teach this skill prior to using this strategy.

Don't think of this as "wasted therapy time," however! When we explain the components of story grammar and demonstrate their role in the story, we help increase students' potential to comprehend both oral and written stories effectively. As an added bonus, this activity also builds vocabulary and helps students become more word conscious.

Method

- ❑ Pre-teach story grammar. This may take several lessons. There are different schemes for story grammar and some can be quite sophisticated and complex. Choose a story grammar scheme that is appropriate for the age/grade/ability level of your students. For elementary grades, I use a basic grammar: setting, characters, problem, action, and resolution. There are more sophisticated story grammar schemes, but I find this particular scheme to be a good place to start.

- ❑ Once students have a general grasp of the elements of a story, create a list of vocabulary words for a specific story or book. Try to include words from tier 2, or even tier 3 for older students. I make sure to include words that would be found in each element and also some words that might work in more than one category—just to make it interesting (e.g. "safe").

- ❑ Next, have the student/s predict in which part of the story each word will appear. I use a chart like the one in the example provided on the following page to provide a visual scaffold. You could complete the chart as an entire class or have each student fill out the chart independently.

- ❑ Then, read the story. You may choose to read it aloud or assign it as an independent reading assignment—whatever is most appropriate for your student or group.

- ❑ Once the story has been read, go back and review the predictions.

When students are provided with a scaffold such as this, both in terms of the story structure and vocabulary words, comprehension often increases. I also find that students pay much more attention—looking for the words that were predicted to see how they did. Of course, you can always add the element of competition if you choose.

Building Better Readers

This example is from one of my favorite chapter book series, *Hank the Cowdog* by John Erickson. This was completed with a group of 4th grade students. Note that some words have question marks next to them. These are words that students identified as potentially being in more than one part of the story. Only after the story was read were they able to determine the final category. I am delighted when students are able to make a case for a word being able to fit more than one category. Sometimes I even award extra points!

Setting	Characters	Problem	Action	Resolution
Texas	Hank	Safe?	Guard?	Safe?
Ranch	Rustlers	Lost	Yelling	Found
Buzzards	Guard?	Rustlers?	Searching	Reward
	Pete the Barn Cat	Calf?		Rescued
	Calf?			

Where do these words fit in this story?

Hank	Ranch	Pete the barn cat
Safe	Guard	Searching
Rustlers	Yelling	Reward
Texas	Found	Lost
Buzzards	Rescued	Calf

Comprehension

DRAW-A-STORY

A common misconception held by many adults (including many educators), is that a student should not be engaged in another task while listening to text being read aloud. This is most likely because they were taught that in order to listen carefully, one must look at the person who is speaking or reading aloud and refrain from doing anything else. Consequently, students are not typically encouraged to draw or doodle while being read to—or while they are supposed to be reading.

However, research shows that the human brain can process information so quickly that simply sitting and listening may actually cause us to drift off task. In a nutshell, our brains become bored and what is being said or read then simply goes "in one ear and out the other." The National Reading Panel report recommends that students be provided with explicit instruction in using mental images, or visualizing, to facilitate comprehension of a reading passage.

One way to help "anchor" students to the text is to allow them to make doodles or draw or otherwise engage their brains as they listen. Depending on their age, I encourage children to "draw what this story makes you think about" or "make a scribble about this story." I might also encourage students to sequence the story through quick illustrations (stick figures work fine) or to draw something that they already know about that has a connection to what is being read (or that they are reading). What they draw isn't particularly important. In fact, I would be careful not to be too rigid in specifying what should be drawn. The point is to let children free-associate to anchor the information to existing cognitive schemas. The fun part is to then allow students to talk about what they drew—and why!

I make an effort to use books that have strong possibilities for visual imagery—this typically means rich vocabulary and an intriguing story line. Here are a few examples to get you started. (You can find more suggestions in the *Comprehension Resources* section of this chapter)

Something From Nothing (Phoebe Gilman)

Baby Joseph eventually outgrows his blue blanket which has begun to wear out. An old tailor recycles it again and again—first into a jacket, then a vest, then a tie, and eventually only enough is left to cover a button. There is a surprising ending that helps the reader think about what it means when we say "something from nothing."

I have used this story successfully with students from Kindergarten through 5th grade. You'll love the pictures of blue coats, ties, buttons, and blankets that are created from the imaginations of your students.

Building Better Readers

Wings (Christopher Myers)

One day, Ikarus Jackson surprises his friends and neighbors by unfolding his "long, strong, proud wings" and flying over the rooftops. Rather than being amazed and awed, he is taunted, and ostracized and, eventually, even kicked out of school. Luckily, one lonely girl decides to find and befriend Ikarus. It isn't easy, but she eventually finds him cowering on a roof with the pigeons. Standing up to his tormentors, she helps him see that being different isn't necessarily bad and declares that his flying is, indeed, "beautiful."

After you read the story and students create their ideas of what Ikarus and his wings might look like, you will want to share the book's gorgeous cut-paper illustrations of the world as seen from the viewpoint of a boy who has wings.

When Lightning Comes in a Jar (Earnest and Patricia Polacco)

Rich in vocabulary and imagery, I have had students start to sketch as soon as I read the title of this book. The story revolves around a family reunion. Actually, it is a story of **two** family reunions—one past and one present. There are "roly-poly" aunties and "zillions of meatloafs" and "gazillions of Jell-O salads." As the title suggests, the day culminates with Gramma showing children how to catch lightning (bugs) in a jar.

So many possibilities for sketching and visualizing that you may find students filling multiple pages with sketches and doodles.

> You can find more books that are rich in visual imagery in the *Comprehension Resources* section of this chapter.

Comprehension

SENSE-O-GRAM

Here is another way to help students engage in the text. It provides a bit more structure than the previous activity, which is necessary for some students, but is still open-ended enough to encourage critical thinking. This activity can be used with a wide variety of students—from early elementary through high school. (In fact, I know a master teacher who uses this very successfully to help high school students learn specific third tier vocabulary related to her field of agri-science).

Method

❑ Read a story or written passage aloud (alternately, older students can be encouraged to read the selected text independently.)

❑ Using the form provided—or your own version—students write words or phrases (or draw a picture) from the story or reading assignment that relates to, or activates, one or all of their five senses.

❑ Students share their sense-o-grams with the rest of the class.

❑ Alternately, students can keep a notebook of all of their sense-o-grams to remind them of what they know about each passage.

✱ **Try reading aloud <u>Night in the Country</u> by Cynthia Rylant. You'll be amazed at what students hear, see, smell, taste, and touch— all from listening to a book.**

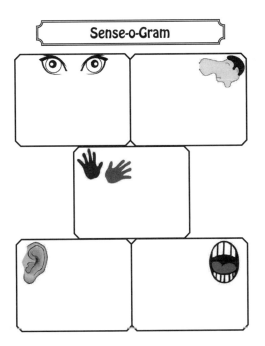

Find a full-sized, reproducible Sense-O-Gram activity sheet in the *Comprehension Resources* of this chapter.

QUESTIONS! QUESTIONS! QUESTIONS!

Asking and answering questions is a core activity for assessing a student's level of comprehension as well as to help students self-monitor their own level of comprehension. There are two kinds of questions that students need to understand in order to maximize their comprehension of written language: 1) questions they ask themselves for comprehension monitoring (I call these "I CAN ASK THAT" questions) and 2) questions asked by others (I call these "I CAN ANSWER THAT" questions). Oftentimes, SLPs are able to assist classroom teachers in determining the kinds of questions that are difficult for specific students and work together with them to design effective instruction to facilitate better comprehension.

I CAN ASK THAT!
(Comprehension Monitoring)

One way readers actively engage in the text is by asking questions before, during, and after they read to clarify fuzzy spots, identify key points, make predictions, and self-assess their understanding of the text. It is extremely important for students to learn to regularly engage in metacognitive self-questioning to help them avoid the trap of thinking they have "read" the assigned text just because they have decoded all (or most) of the words. I find it helpful to clue students in on the fact that if they learn to ask the right kinds of questions of **themselves** the questions that **teachers** ask on tests or during oral quizzes will be much easier to answer!

You can help students learn to flex their metacognitive muscles by explicitly teaching them the kinds of questions that they should be asking themselves before, during, and after reading. Some suggestions are provided below. (Note that some of these are covered by the activities outlined in this chapter).

SAMPLE SELF-QUESTIONS TO ASK PRIOR TO READING

- ❖ What is my purpose for reading this text passage? (See **What's my Purpose** activity provided in this chapter)
- ❖ What is the author's purpose for writing this text passage? (See **Name that Purpose** activity provided in this chapter)
- ❖ What do I already know about the topic?
- ❖ Is there new vocabulary that I have recently learned that I should pay attention to?
- ❖ Are there answers to questions that I know will be asked about this text that I should be looking for?

Comprehension

SAMPLE SELF-QUESTIONS TO ASK DURING READING*

- ❖ Does this make sense?
- ❖ Do I understand all the words?
- ❖ What is the topic?
- ❖ Can I identify the main idea?
- ❖ How does this relate to my life or something I already know?

✹ *Suggestion:* Use the "Here's What I Think" activity provided in this chapter to model comprehension monitoring via self-questioning during reading.

SAMPLE SELF-QUESTIONS TO ASK AFTER READING

Be able to answer all of the questions in the first two categories, PLUS:

- ❖ Can I summarize the key points or plot features?
- ❖ Are there words I still don't understand?
- ❖ How does this information relate to what I already know?
- ❖ Do I need to read other material or sections of the text to provide missing information?
- ❖ Have I formed an opinion about what I read? What is it?
- ❖ What questions do I still have about this passage?

I CAN ANSWER THAT!
(Understanding Questions Asked by Others)

In addition to asking themselves the right questions to maximize comprehension during reading, students need to be able to give the right answer to demonstrate their comprehension to others. This can be intimidating, particularly when students don't understand that there are different kinds of questions that require different kinds of answers.

Building Better Readers

RIGHT-THERE QUESTIONS

Right-There questions are those for which the answers can be found right in the text, typically in a single sentence. Sometimes referred to as text-explicit questions, these questions require a concrete answer that is typically either correct or incorrect (close-ended questions). Classic Wh- questions are examples of **Right-There Questions**. Students need to know that if they cannot remember the answer to a question of this type, they can typically find the answer simply by re-reading the text.

- ❖ **Right There Questions typically use terms such as:** *Who, What, When, Where, List, Name.*

- ❖ **Typical Use on Exams:** *True or False, Fill in the Blank, Multiple Choice, Word Bank*

THINK-ABOUT-IT QUESTIONS

These types of questions, that require an answer based on information from more than one sentence in the text, are sometimes referred to as text-implicit questions. These are open-ended questions that require students to infer or synthesize information rather than merely provide a rote answer.

- ❖ **Think-About-it-Questions typically use terms such as:** *Why, Summarize, Compare, Contrast, Explain, or Retell*

- ❖ **Typical Use on Exams:** *Essay or Short Answer Questions*

WHAT-I-KNOW-AND-THINK-MATTERS QUESTIONS

Another type of open-ended questions, the answers to this third type of question are not found in the text at all. They require the student to tap into their prior knowledge of the subject or some aspect of their life that relates to the text. (These are sometimes called scriptal questions).

- ❖ **What-I-Know-and-Think-Matters Questions ask students to:** *Reflect, Predict, or Provide an opinion.*

- ❖ **Typically found on a test as:** *Essay question*

Comprehension

TOP TEN WAYS TO IMPROVE YOUR READING

Some students may find it helpful to have a summary of self-activating strategies available to use as a reference during reading interactions. You can turn this into a *brainstorm-discuss-synthesize-implement* activity or you could just provide the list of strategies, discuss them, and then concentrate on helping students learn to use the reference consistently and appropriately.

You can put this reference into any form, but I have had good luck with a bookmark. Of course, with the rapid advances we are witnessing in e-book technology, bookmarks may soon be as relevant as a typewriter. Perhaps you'll just want to create an app for that!

Here are the strategies that I typically use as my "Top Ten Ways to Improve Your Reading." You and your students may come up with different top-ten strategies (or even more than ten). The critical thing is to help students realize that there are strategies that they can use when they get stuck—and that "give up" is *not* one of them.

READING SUCCESS STRATEGIES

• • • • • •

1. Identify a purpose
2. Read and re-read
3. Look at headings and pictures
4. Create a mental image
5. Define unknown words
6. Ask questions
7. Think about what you already know
8. Think about what you don't know
9. Summarize what you read
10. Ask for help

• • • • • •

Full-sized, reproducible versions of this bookmark can be found in the *Comprehension Resources* section of this chapter.

Building Better Readers

SQR3

We now have evidence to support the use of this strategy which I started using more than 25 years ago when I was working with students in the public schools. (I learned this technique from the teacher for students with Learning Disabilities at Decorah Elementary School in West Bend, Wisconsin. Thanks for sharing, Bonnie!) I find it works especially well with middle and high-school students, although I have used it with some upper-elementary level students as well. It is also appropriate for use with adults.

The strength of this technique is that it provides a scaffold or framework for reading text that facilitates comprehension. It also provides a purpose and, if done correctly, thoroughly and actively engages the student in the reading.

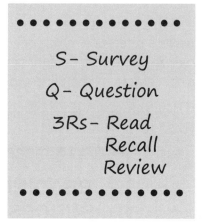

S– Survey
Q– Question
3Rs– Read
   Recall
   Review

S SURVEY (OR SKIM)

Prior to reading the passage and to create a context for reading,

▶ *The title and introduction*

▶ *Key words*

▶ *Main headings and subheadings*

▶ *Figures and/or graphs, including the caption*

▶ *Summaries or study questions*

Comprehension

 QUESTION

While surveying, formulate questions about the text such as:

▶ *What is this written passage (chapter, story, assignment) about?*

▶ *What question is this written passage trying to answer?*

▶ *What do I already know about this topic?*

▶ *How does this information help me?*

▶ *What is my purpose for reading this text?*

> **See *Questions! Questions! Questions!* Activity for a more extensive list of questions**

 READ

Employ active reading strategies while you read the written passage:

▶ *Look for answers to the questions you developed.*

▶ *Answer questions at the beginning or end of chapters or study guides.*

▶ *Study all graphics—charts, figures, graphs, pictures, etc.*

▶ *Reread all captions.*

▶ *Note all the underlined, italicized, bold printed words or phrases.*

▶ *Monitor comprehension. As necessary:*

  o *Reduce your speed for difficult passages.*

  o *Stop and reread parts which are not clear.*

  o *Break passage into smaller chunks rather than trying to read it all at once.*

Building Better Readers

(R2) RECALL (OR RECITE)

Immediately after reading the written passage (in whole or in part):

▶ *Answer the questions formulated in the Q phase.*

▶ *Summarize what was read orally or in writing.*

▶ *Underline or highlight new vocabulary words and/or key points.*

▶ *Compare and contrast information found in this passage to what you already knew or thought you knew.*

(R3) REVIEW

This is an on-going process and is the antidote to the "cram and jam" technique that so many students default to because they don't how to study effectively. Students who learn to review every day do not have to engage in "panic study" or try to rely on rote memorization of random facts. Routinely using these review techniques on a regular, on-going basis facilitates a deeper, more diversified level of comprehension.

▶ *Review notes, study guides, and other class material.*

▶ *Participate actively in classroom discussions.*

▶ *Re-read text passages several times.*

▶ *Attempt to recall meaning of new or specialized vocabulary and/or key phrases.*

▶ *Create an outline or a semantic web of the targeted material—first with resources available and then from memory.*

▶ *Ask and answer your own questions about the material.*

READING COMPREHENSION RESOURCES

Comprehension Resources

WORDLESS BOOKS

A Boy, A Dog, and a Frog (series)	Mercer Meyer
Chalk	Bill Thompson
Changes, Changes	Pat Hutchins
The Chicken Thief	Beatrice Rodriquez
A Circle of Friends	Giora Carmi
Deep in the Forest	Brindon Turkle
Good Dog, Carl (series)	Alexandra Day
Good Night, Gorilla	Emily Arnold McCullah
Flotsam	David Weisner
The Grey Lady and the Strawberry Snatcher	Molly Bang
Home	Jeannie Baker
The Lion and the Mouse	Jerry Pinkney
Looking Down	Steven Jenkins
Mirror	Jeannie Baker
Museum Trip	Barbara Lehman
The Polar Bear Waltz	Outside Magazine
Rainstorm	Barbara Lehman
The Red Book	Barbara Lehman

Building Better Readers

Rooster's Revenge	Beatrice Rodriquez
Sector Seven	David Weisner
Sidewalk Circus	Paul Fleischman
The Silver Pony	Lynd Ward
Trainstop	Barbara Lehman
Tuesday	David Weisner
Wave	Susie Lee
Will's Mammoth	Rafe Martin
Window	Jeannie Baker

BOOKS THAT ENCOURAGE COMPREHENSION THROUGH PREDICTING, VISUALIZING, AND PROBLEM SOLVING

The Bee Tree	Patricia Polacco
Finn Family Moomintroll	Tove Jansson
It Could Always Be Worse	Margot Zemich
Main Ideas & Summarizing: 35 Reading Passages for Comprehension	Linda Ward Beech
My Father's Hands	Joanne Ryder
The Name Jar	Yangsook Choi

Comprehension Resources

Night in the Country	Cynthia Rylant
Nonfiction Comprehension Cliffhangers: 15 High-Interest True Stories That Invite Students to Infer, Visualize, and Summarize to Predict the Ending of Each Story	Tom Conklin
The Other Side	Jacqueline Woodson
Seven Blind Mice	Ed Young
Short Cut	David Macaulay
Spotless Spot*	Alexandra Crouse
Two Mice in Three Fables	Lynn Reisen
When Lightning Comes in a Jar	Earnest and Patricia Polacco
Wings	Christopher Myers
The Wolf Who Cried Boy	Bob Hartman
What Do you Do with a Tail Like This?	Steve Jenkins
Wilfrid Gordon McDonald Partridge	Mem Fox

* **Available from Dynamic Resources**

Building Better Readers

WHAT'S MY PURPOSE?

Text Selection _____
(example: title of book, chapter, article, page range, etc)

- ☐ Read for pleasure
- ☐ Read to learn new vocabulary
- ☐ Read to be able to discuss with others
- ☐ Read to learn a procedure
- ☐ Read to find answers
- ☐ Read for specific information
- ☐ Read to compare and contrast
- ☐ Read and reflect
- ☐ Read and summarize
- ☐ Other _____

■ ■

NOTES

Comprehension Resources

Text _____

My Purpose for Reading This Selection

- ☐ Read for pleasure
- ☐ Read to learn new vocabulary
- ☐ Read to be able to discuss with others
- ☐ Read to learn a procedure
- ☐ Read to find answers
- ☐ Read for specific information
- ☐ Read to compare and contrast
- ☐ Read and reflect
- ☐ Read and summarize
- ☐ Other _____

- -

The Author's Purpose for Writing this Selection

- ☐ Tell a Story
- ☐ Compare and Contrast
- ☐ Convince an audience
- ☐ Convey information
- ☐ Entertain
- ☐ Report and inform
- ☐ Share an experience
- ☐ Other _____

Reproducible for Educational Use-Dynamic Resources

Building Better Readers

Predict-A-Story

Setting	Characters	Problem	Action	Resolution

Where do these words fit in this story?

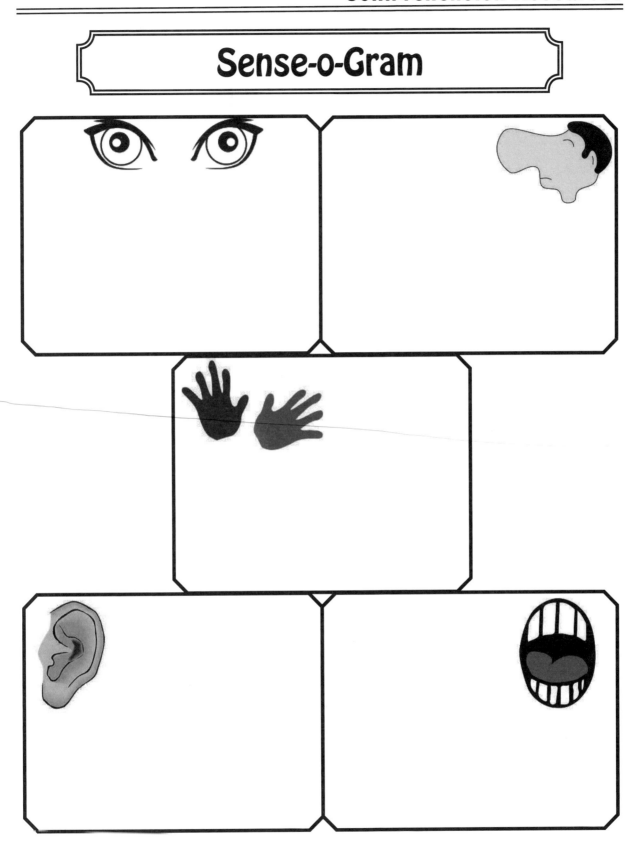

Building Better Readers

Reading for Success Bookmarks

READING SUCCESS STRATEGIES

• • • • • •

1. Identify a purpose
2. Read and re-read
3. Look at headings and pictures
4. Create a mental image
5. Define unknown words
6. Ask questions
7. Think about what you already know
8. Think about what you don't know
9. Summarize what you read
10. Ask for help

• • • • • •

READING SUCCESS STRATEGIES

• • • • • •

1. Identify a purpose
2. Read and re-read
3. Look at headings and pictures
4. Create a mental image
5. Define unknown words
6. Ask questions
7. Think about what you already know
8. Think about what you don't know
9. Summarize what you read
10. Ask for help

• • • • • •

CHAPTER 7

Building Better Readers

The Motivation to Read!

Hopefully, if you have worked your way through this resource and reached this chapter, it's because YOU are truly motivated to building your students into better readers. And while each of the skills discussed so far is critical to literacy development, there is more to building better readers than simply teaching a set of specific skills. In fact, the **motivation to read** has been identified by the National Reading Panel as the final component in effective reading instruction.

The research is clear in demonstrating a strong correlation between *how much* a student reads and *how well* they read. In other words, the best readers read the most and poorest readers read the least. While we can't claim that reading more CAUSES children to be better readers, it IS possible that that better readers may simply choose to read more (because they enjoy it).

If you have attended any of my workshops on literacy, you know that I am a big proponent of helping children who have lost—or never developed—the joy of reading to begin to discover the magic they can find in books. Because so many of the students on our caseloads struggle with reading, it is not uncommon to hear them make negative statements about reading. ("It's boring." "I hate to read." "I'm too tired to read now.") They do not consider themselves readers and, as a result, tend to read much less than their classmates.

> *The best readers read the most and the poorest readers read the least.*
>
> ~National Reading Panel

Further, students who struggle with oral and written language have been described as suffering from the "Matthew effect" in which, "the rich get richer and the poor get poorer". From this perspective, good readers read more and become better readers resulting in a higher motivation to read more. (I think of this as a positive reading spiral.) Conversely, poor readers read less and, because they are exposed to less written language, become poorer readers who, in turn, become more and more reluctant to read (a negative reading spiral).

Helping struggling students find their motivation to read can be a challenge. However, there are a number of strategies that we can employ to help reluctant readers discover that reading can be a rewarding activity. Our goal is to replace the feelings of dread and avoidance with anticipation and pleasure. No small feat, but doable!

The first, and most important, step in encouraging unmotivated students to read is to get their noses in a book. *ANY* book …..of *ANY* level …. of *ANY* genre that piques their interest. Over the years, I have found that there are some types of books—and some books in specific—that work especially well in helping reluctant readers find their way to the realization that reading can fun. I have shared a few in the following pages. (You'll find more in the *Resources* section of this chapter.)

Building Better Readers

EYE CANDY
(ENGAGING VISUAL LEARNERS)

Many of the children on speech/language caseloads do not process information efficiently through the auditory mode (which is very likely why they are on your caseload). Unfortunately, strongly visual learners are not typically well-supported in regular education classrooms where a great deal of the information is presented orally. Students are expected to listen, process, and assimilate it into their cognitive schemas using primarily the auditory mode. This can be extremely discouraging for visual learners who typically blame themselves for their learning difficulties and may easily give up on themselves in the academic setting. So, I look for oppotunities to show visual learners that there are books for them, too!

Visual learners will be drawn to books that include a high level of detail and/or include unexpected ways to look at objects. Once we have them "hooked" on the visual aspect of the book, the words become tools that allow these students to learn more about the visual content— which is what really interests them. My son, a visual learner if there ever was one, spent hours lost in Where's Waldo and other similar books. (Personally, "Waldo" gave me a headache and I really didn't care WHERE he was. But for him, this was pure joy.) He eventually graduated into Joan Steiner's Look-Alikes books and then Steve Biesty's Cross Sections series where he would read incredible amounts of fine print text to discover what was going on in the pictures. Other visual learners I have worked with demonstrated a similar pattern. Once they discovered that reading can involve all sorts of fun visual detail, they were much more willing to engage in text.

Here is a sampling of some of my favorite books for visual learners. I strongly suggest you try out a few with the students who just don't seem to be interested in reading. You may find that once they understand that *looking* at a book is not only allowed but encouraged, their motivation to read increases.

Look-Alikes (Joan Steiner)

The catch phrase for this wonderful series of books, *"The more you look, the more you see,"* aptly sums up what students (adults, too) will experience as they pore over these books. Hundreds of "found" objects are used to create three-dimensional everyday scenes. At first glance, they look exactly like one would expect them to look—but a more detailed inspection yields surprising findings.

For instance, in the "street" scene (one of my favorites), a bus stop sign is actually a meat thermometer, a sweater with buttons serves as a store front. In other scenes, a shoehorn fills in very nicely as a slide and real human hair forms the golden curtains for the Nutcracker ballet. These scenes (which are truly works of genius) provide a virtual smorgasbord of engagement opportunities for visual learners of all ages who will want to read all the fine print in the back of the book to find out "how she did that!"

The Motivation to Read!

Fun with Hand Shadows (Sati Achath)

This book not only engages visual learners (and just about every other student I've ever worked with), it provides the reader with a pragmatically useful party skill. ☺ Just as the title suggests, the author, a shadow puppeteer, ventriloquist, and magician, shares all of his secrets about how to create some of the most amazing hand shadows you can imagine. Visual learners are motivated to read the directions to discover how to create all sorts of shadow silouettes—from the simple "deer roaming the forest" (even I can do this one) to "kicking donkey" and "the big elephant." There are even directions for portraying historical figures (e.g., George Washington) and celebrities (e.g., Jay Leno).

If you really want to get kids motivated, haul out a desk lamp, free up some wall space, and let your visual learners show of their skills. They will soon be teaching YOU how to have "fun with hand shadows!"

How are you Peeling? (Saxton Freyman and Joost Alphers)

The "naturally expressive" fruits and vegetables photographed for this book are laugh-out-loud funny as they portray a range of emotions using only positioning and two chick peas for eyes to enhance their natural shapes. Happy, sad, shy, mad, lonely, angry – there is lots of room for lively discussion in addition to the rhyming text that accompanies each tableau.

✷ **You may also want to try <u>Food for Thought</u> and <u>Fast Food</u> by the same author.**

Zoom (Marvin Terban)

This book actually fits into both the "wordless book" and "books that fascinate visual learners" categories. It starts with a close-up of a colorful, roughly-triangular object that could be any number of things. On the next page, the perspective recedes, as if the viewer has taken two steps back (or the camera has "zoomed out"), so that more of the illustration is revealed. The change in perspective typically then requires readers to change their OWN perspective as surprising new visual elements are revealed.

Typically, visual learners are hooked immediately and can't wait to see what is going to "happen" next. There are also multiple opportunities for predicting and critical thinking.

✷ **Students who are intrigued by <u>Zoom</u> will probably also like <u>Re-Zoom</u> by the same author.**

Building Better Readers

Cross Sections Series (Steven Biesty)

In this series, cut-away illustrations reveal the inner workings and infrastructure of buildings, machines, vehicles, places, and even the human body. Locomotives, helicopters, ocean liners, Spanish galleons, subway stations, jets —each is revealed from the inside out with incredible detail. But this isn't merely an intricate picture book. It is also absolutely PACKED with details, explanations, and facts about each object. So, as they peruse the details of an observatory, readers also learn about how reflected light forms an image at the Cassegrain focus point, that the massive telescope rides on bearings that must be supported by pressurized oil, and that observatory workers eat their main meals in the middle of the night.

This series is aimed at older readers—fourth grade or so through high school. My now-adult son probably owns every one of the books in this series, including the entire Star Wars Cross Sections line. (Someone with extraordinary imagination actually created interiors, details, and facts for things such as star fighters, the death star, land speeders, and Imperial Walkers.) These books are truly a visual learner's candy store and I highly recommend them.

Mirror, Mirror: A Book of Reversible Verse (Marilyn Singer)

This book is so unique that it is almost impossible to explain. It is a collection of poems based on well-known fairy tales such as Little Red Riding Hood, Snow White, Rapunzel, Hansel and Gretel, and the like. Each story is represented as a poem—but not just ANY poem. These literary marvels can be read both forward and backward, being, in effect, "mirror images" of one another. The amazing thing is that they make sense in both directions. Here is a sample of a *reverso* poem (as termed by the author), from the book:

The Road

It may be such	You need to go
a fairy tale secret	wherever
this much	the road leads -
I know;	I know
The road leads	this much
wherever	A fairy tale secret?
you need to go	It may be such.

Some are short—some are longer. All are remarkably engaging and truly amazing! Your visual learners will enjoy figuring out how the poem works from all angles. This book is also great for building vocabulary and facilitating reading fluency.

The Motivation to Read!

FOR LAUGHING OUT LOUD

Now we come to my favorite category of all—**humor**! Laughing and learning are not mutually exclusive. In fact, humor, at its core, is a highly linguistic construct. Puns, double meanings, and word play often are the crux of making something "funny" so children who learn about humor typically are also building language, vocabulary, and comprehension as well. For instance, children who don't understand ambiguity don't laugh when someone is admiring a new baby and says to the mother, "I didn't know you had it in you!"

> *Don't be afraid to laugh in therapy. It's good for our students—and for us!*

A perfectly good reason to read is to be *entertained*. Consequently, we can use funny books to engage students and help reinforce that reading can be a pleasurable experience. If students think of reading as work—it IS work. So, if we truly want to build a *reader*, we can help students capture the joy of reading by showing them that turning a page might just bring a laugh or an unexpected giggle.

Humorous books challenge readers to think about **why** they are funny. I look for books with unexpected story lines, funny pictures, a tempting "gimmick", or wholesome zaniness. In a nutshell, books that that are just plain fun to read.

Here are a few of my laugh-out-loud favorites with proven track records of getting noses into books. (You can find more in the *Resources* section of this chapter.)

Shark vs Train (Chris Barton)

In this fabulous, fun romp through imagination, two boys run for the toy box. One pulls out a toy shark and the other a train. In the grand tradition of boys, they decide to have a competition to see which one will win. But, of course that depends on the competition. Underwater—it's a shark (fins down). On a see-saw, train sends shark flying. Train wins the belching contest; but shark prevails in the pie-eating race. But who wins if they are playing hide and seek, or facing off in a video game, or exploring distant galaxies? Students can let their imaginations run wild and, of course, create many new scenarios for shark and train—as well as other "toy box" match-ups.

Building Better Readers

Dos and Don'ts (Todd Parr)

This is an elegantly simple little book that can be used with students from kindergarten through the upper grades. On one page is a "Do" and on the facing page is a matching "Don't."

For instance

- DO….pick up your socks, but DON'T…..make anyone smell them.

The fun part is to read the book aloud and have students try to come up with a "don't" to go along with the "do." They don't have to guess what the author said to be "right.". They only need to come up with something that is somehow related.

For instance

- DO….help clean up the house, but DON'T…. (These examples from real-live students.)
    - Scrub the paint off the walls
    - Mess the house back up
    - Build a mountain out of the dust-fluffies
    - Put soap in the toilet
    - (The author's suggestion?" "Don't vacuum up the cat.")

The Stinky Cheeseman and Other Fairly Stupid Tales (Jon Sciezak)

Aimed squarely at upper-elementary and middle-school students, this is a collection of "fractured" fairy tales very loosely based on well-known tales such as the Ugly Duckling (in this version, he doesn't grow to be a swan, just a really ugly duck) and the princess who kissed a frog (but here she ends up without a prince, only slimy frog lips). The stories themselves are quite short—helping to keep the interest of even the most reluctant of readers—and there is a good selection without creating a sense of being overwhelmed by choice. The author also plays with the whole concept of a "book" and the characters show up in each other's stories seemingly at will. No page is safe from his wackiness—the table of contents is mixed up and even the copyright page doesn't follow the "rules."

The Motivation to Read!

The Diary of A Wombat (Jackie French)

Who knew that wombats kept diaries? (Actually, who knew that a wombat was a creature who is a little smaller than a bear who lives in Australia in a hole in the ground, sleeps most of the day, and likes the "occasional treat?") The diary starts simply enough with the day of the week at the top and entries like:

> MORNING: Slept
>
> AFTERNOON: Slept
>
> EVENING: Slept.
>
> NIGHT: Ate grass.

This soon changes when a family moves into the wombat's neighborhood and she discovers the joys of having a human clan nearby. Her encounters with "flat dusty objects" (their welcome mat), "large metal objects" (trash cans), and "delicious treats" (carrots out of their garden and eventually the grocery bag) will keep readers giggling and thinking about how everyday objects might look different to a wombat. There are several other books in the series. I laugh every time I read them—perhaps you'll enjoy them too.

Interrupting Chicken (David Ezra Stein)

Every time Papa Chicken tries to read a bedtime story to Little Red Chicken, she gets so excited that she interrupts the story to warn the characters about what is going to happen next. Papa chastises her to "not get so involved" because she is supposed to be relaxing to go to sleep. Having no luck, he eventually has Little Chicken tell a bedtime story—with surprising results.

Naked Mole Rat Gets Dressed (Mo Willems)

I started laughing at this book the first time I read the title. With a story written about a society of Naked Mole Rats (yes, there is such a creature), how can the book be anything but funny? When a young Naked Mole Rat suddenly gets a hankering to wear clothes, the colony is perplexed, appalled, and sarcastic—especially when he tries to open a clothing store. Finally, with the simple question "why not?" the colony of naked mole rats embraces the possibilities of fashion as outlet for personal expression.

Building Better Readers

The Everything Kids Joke Book

This is a joke book for kids 9-12. There is lots of great humor in the form of limericks, puns, knock-knock jokes, nickname games, riddles, and plain old "groaners." But there is more to this book than just reading jokes. It also teaches kids how to create jokes of their own, how to TELL them, and how to get laughs. There are multiple opportunities to learn new vocabulary and solve riddles – plenty of motivation to exercise reading skills.

> **Find additional books, websites, and activities to motivate and inspire your students in the *Motivation Resources* section of this chapter!**

NOW THAT'S FUNNY

Another way to incorporate humor into therapy is to mine the internet for crazy pictures and encourage students to create captions that make a funny picture even funnier. This requires appropriate use of vocabulary, an understanding of the premise of a pun, knowledge of double meaning words, and other higher level linguistic concepts.

For instance: Here are some captions provided by students for this picture:

* *"Did I do that?"*

* *"I hate it when that happens!"*

* *"He just cracked under the pressure."*

* *"EWWWW!"*

One of my favorite examples of this involves a picture of a rather rotund cat who has tried to fit herself into a round basket that is about two sizes too small. As a result, a substantial amount of her is spilling over all around the rim of the basket. The student's caption?

"MUFFIN TOP!!"

> Try **www.icanhasacheeseburger** for funny pictures you might use for this activity.

HALF-BAKED HEADLINES

Another strategy is to bring in funny headlines, advertisements, or slogans and have the students try to figure out what makes them funny. Here are some examples:

Headlines

- *Police Begin Campaign To Run Down Jaywalkers*

- *Blind Woman Gets New Kidney from Dad She Hasn't Seen in Years*

- *Red Tape Holds Up New Bridge*

Advertisements/Slogans

- *Welcome to Curl Up 'N Dye Hair Salon!*

- *"I love you only" Valentine cards: Now available in multi-packs.*

- *We do not tear your clothing with machinery. We do it carefully by hand.*

- *This car is protected by an anti-theft sticker.*

Being able to recognize that these are funny—and then identify WHY—taps into higher-level linguistic processing and vocabulary knowledge. Consequently, students can truly "laugh and learn."

Extension/Variations

- Encourage students to look for their own funny ads, headlines, signs, etc. I actually have had students submit their finds to televised talk shows—and several had their submissions shared on local and national television. Now, THAT'S a motivation for reading!

- **(More Advanced)** Have students come up with their own "half-baked headlines" and then have them create the story that goes along with it.

FIGURATIVE LANGUAGE

Although the topic of figurative language could be addressed under both vocabulary and comprehension (because it affects, and is a component of, both skills), I include it in this chapter because it can truly be a lot fun—as well as important building block to better reading.

It seems a little unfair that a child can learn the meaning of a word or phrase, but then find out it doesn't actually mean what the words suggest! English is an incredibly figurative language that includes numerous examples of non-literacy language such as:

Smilies   *He's as healthy as a horse*

Metaphors   *The car is a lemon*

Proverbs   *A stitch in time saves nine*

Idioms   *It's raining cats and dogs*

You can, of course, address figurative meaning through direct instruction of these constructs, but it's so much more fun to use books to facilitate an understanding of non-literal language.

Here are some of my favorite books that faciliate an understanding of figurative language. (You'll find a more extensive list in the *Motivation Resources* section of this chapter)

Quick as a Cricket (Audrey Wood)

This book stands out because it is chock-full of smilies with wonderful illustrations that help the reader see the logic behind the comparison. For instance, "I'm strong as an ox" depicts the child pulling a cart in tandem with a very muscular representation of that particular creature. You'll also find "I'm happy as a lark," I'm large as a whale," I'm gentle as a lamb," and "I'm busy as a bee." ("Put them all together and you'll have me!")

This is also an excellent book to read using Echo and/or Paired reading. It is also effective for building reading fluency, vocabulary, and comprehension right along with figurative language.

Building Better Readers

Squids will be Squids: Fresh Morals, Beastly Fables (Jon Scieszka)

Written in the spirit of Aesop's fables, complete with proverbs following each vignette, this is a funny romp that is great for middle-school students and older. With a cast of charactors that includes termites, a musk-ox, fleas, and a duck-billed platypus, these are the fables Aesop "might have told if he were alive today and sitting in the back of the class daydreaming and goofing around instead of paying attention and doing his homework…."

Judge Judy's Cool Rules for School (Judy Scheinlin)

I would be remiss if I didn't mention my favorite figurative language resource for upper elementary through high school students. (Yes, it is written by THAT Judge Judy). In this book, she provides an idiom and then illustrates the meaning through a short paragraph and a multiple choice "quiz." The fun part is that several of the foils are responses that many students of this age would actually consider. For instance, in response to a bad report card, choice d) is: "add a plus sign to every grade." There is no answer key, so students can be encouraged to discuss each vignette in terms of which response most accurately reflects the meaning of the idiom and its consequences in real life situations.

There are more than 25 idioms presented in this book. Enough for an entire semester- or longer!

> **Find more books for facilitating figurative language in the *Motivation Resources* secton of this chapter.**

The Motivation to Read!

FRACTURED FIGURATIVE LANGUAGE!

I was inspired to create this activity by one of those "this is funny" emails that I get from time to time from colleagues and friends. The activity involved giving Kindergartners the first half of an idiom and asking them to complete it. The results were pretty hilarious. Here are some examples: (You can find the entire list in the *Motivation Resources* section of this chapter)

- **A penny saved is………………………not much.**
- **Never underestimate the power of……….termites.**
- **You can lead a horse to water but………how?**
- **Happy the bride who…………………..gets all the presents.**

Method

- Review the list of "fractured figurative language" (See the **Motivation Resources** section of this chapter) and talk about why they are funny.

- Have students create a similar task by creating a figurative language fill-in-the blank quiz of their own. They will need to research figurative language to do this! (Check out the books in the **Motivation Resources** section related to figurative language as potential sources).

- Don't limit the quiz to idioms only. Similies (*hungry as a……….*) and proverbs (*A stitch in time saves……*) also work well.

- Have students interview others and record the results. Try to get responses from students across a variety of age/grade levels.

- Talk about what you discovered. Compare and contrast responses. Were some of the sayings better known than others? If someone didn't know the idiom, did they just make it up? Were there any really funny responses?

Extension/Variations

- Create different quizzes for different ages. Try to come up with some really tough ones for adults.

- Create your own "Fractured Figurative Language" book and share with others!

READING CIRCLES

Anyone who has ever tried to reach a goal—such as losing weight or learning a new language—knows that you become **much** more motivated to work toward that goal when held accountable by others. Reading circles work the same way. They harness the proven power of group energy to encourage students to become, and remain, engaged and motivated to read.

Reading Circles are an effective way to help counteract the learned helplessness that is so often seen in middle and high school students who struggle with language and learning. Rather than teaching them to rely on an adult, students engaged in Reading Circles learn to rely on themselves and each other to learn and grow. As a group, students are encouraged to take control over their reading by choosing what they read, how many pages they will read each day, and how they will respond individually to the selection. They then meet as a group to discuss their personal responses.

The teacher or SLP is not a part of the reading circle. They merely function as an observer and occasional advisor. It is up to the group to keep each other motivated and engaged.

The best way to support success is to provide students with some basic tools—such as guidelines for participation, a list of questions to guide a discussion, tasks to extend reading, and sample reading contracts. The group can choose to use what you provide, modify it, or create their own.

There are a number of quality websites devoted to reading circles that can provide you with more extensive background related to reading circles as well as suggested literacy activities and books broken down by grade level. I have provided some suggested sites in the resources section that follows.

Websites that provide information and resources for Reading/ Literacy Circles can be found in the *Motivation Resources* section of this chapter.

MOTIVATION RESOURCES

Motivation Resources

BOOKS FOR VISUAL LEARNERS

Alphabet City	Stephen Johnson
Beautiful Oops!	Barney Saltzberg
Bones	Steven Jenkins
Boo to a Goose	Mem Fox
Changes, Changes	Pat Hutchins
City By Numbers	Stephen Johnson
Cross Sections (series)	Steven Bietsy
Doodlebug	Ross Collins
Dot	Peter H. Reynolds
Duck! Rabbit!	Amy Krouse Rosenthal
Eye Popping Optical Illusions	Michael Dispezio
Fun with Hand Shadows	Sati Achath
Green	Laura Vaccaro Seeger
Home (wordless)	Jennie Baker
How are you Peeling? Foods with Moods	Saxton Freyman
How Would You Survive in Ancient Greece?	Fiona MacDonald & Mark Bergen
How Would You Survive in the Middle Ages?	Fiona MacDonald
King Bidgood's in the Bathtub	Audry Wood

Building Better Readers

Lines that Wiggle	Candace Whitman
Look-Alikes Series	Joan Steiner
Looking Down	Steven Jenkins
The Look Book	Tana Hoban
Look! Look! Look!	Tana Hoban
Marvelous Mazes	Juliet Snape
Mirror (wordless)	Jeannie Baker
Mirror, Mirror: A Book of Reversible Verse	Marilyn Singer
Mom and Dad are Pallidromes	Marvin Tervan
Mouse Mess	Linnea Riley
Museum ABC	Metropolitan Museum of Art
Optical Illusion Magic	Michael Dispazio
Optical Tricks	Walter Wick
The Paper Crane	Molly Bang
Prairie Town	Arthur Geisert
Reflections	Ana Jonas
Re-Zoom	Istvan Banyal
River Town	Arthur Beisert
Round Trip	Ana Jonas
Seven Blind Mice	Ed Young

Motivation Resources

Shadow	Suzy Lee
Shadows and Reflections	Tana Hoban
Star Wars Incredible Cross Sections	David West Reynolds
Something's Not Quite Right	Guy Billout
Two Bad Ants	Chris Van Allsberg
The Three Pigs	David Wiesner
Tickets to Ride: An Alphabetic Amusement	Mark Rogalski
The Ultimate Book of Optical Illusion	Al Seckel
Window (wordless)	Jeannie Baker
Zoom	Islvan Banyai

BOOKS FOR FIGURATIVE LANGUAGE

Amelia Bedelia	Peggy Parish
Chocolate Moose for Dinner	Fred Gwynne,
Crazy Like a Fox	Lorren Leedy
Duck for President	Doreen Cronin
Even More Parts	Tedd Arnold
Giggle, Giggle, Quack	Doreen Cronin
In a Pickle and other Funny Idioms	Marvin Terban

Building Better Readers

It Figures	Marvin Terban
The King Who Rained	Fred Gwynne
Mad as a Wet Hen	Marvin Terban
More Parts	Tedd Arnold
Quick as a Cricket	Audrey Woods
Squids will be Squids	Jon Scieszka
Stubborn as a Mule and Other Silly Similes	Nancy Jean Loewen
You Can't Judge a Book By It's Cover (Cool Rules for School)	Judith Scheinlen
You're Toast and Other Metaphors we Adore	Nancy Jean Loewen
Why the Banana Split	Rick Walton

JUST FOR FUN BOOKS

A Bad Day at Riverbend	Chris Van Allsberg
Bones	Steven Jenkins
The Adventures of Taxi Dog	Debra Barracca
Animals Should Definitely Not Wear Clothing	Judy Barrett
Can't Sleep Without Sheep	Susanna Leonard Hill
Chicken Big	Keith Graves
Children Make Terrible Pets	Peter Brown

Motivation Resources

CinderEdna	Ellen Jackson
Dear Peter Rabbit	Alma Flor Ada
Diary of a Fly	Doreen Cronin
Diary of a Spider	Doreen Cronin
Diary of a Worm	Doreen Cronin
Diary of a Wombat	Jackie French
Diary of a Baby Wombat	Jackie French
Dos and Don'ts	Todd Parr
Duck at the Door	Jackie Urbanovic
Duck, Duck, Moose	Dave Horowitz
Ella, Of Course	Sarah Weeks
The Everything Kids Joke Book	Michael Dahl
Falling for Rapuzel	Leah Wilcox
Fancy Nancy (Series)	Jane O'Connor
The Fantastic Flying Books of Mr. Morris Lessmore	William Joyce
Fast and Slow: Poems for Advanced Children and Beginning Parents	John Ciardi
Flamingos on the Roof: Poems and Paintings	Calef Brown
Fly Guy Series	Todd Arnold
The Frog Prince Continued	Jon Scieszka
Grandpa's Teeth	Rod Clement

Building Better Readers

Hank the Cowdog (Series)	John Erickson
The Hidden Alphabet	Laura Vaccaro Seeger
I Ain't Gonna Paint No More	Karen Beaumont
Interrupting Chicken	David Ezra Stein
If I Were a Lion	Sarah Weeks
The Jolly Postman: Or Other People's Letters	Janet Ahlberg
Just Joking	National Geographic Kids
Miss Nelson is Missing	Harry Allard & James Marshall
Meerkat Mail	Emily Gravett
Memories of Goldfish	Devin Scillan
Monsters Eat Whiny Children	Bruce Eric Kaplan
Olive, the Other Reindeer	J. Otto Seibold
Naked Mole Rat Gets Dressed	Mo Williams
Never, Ever Shout in a Zoo	Karma Wilson
The Night I Followed my Dog	Nina Laden
Olive, My Love	J. Otto Seibolt
Parts	Todd Arnold
Pierre the Penguin	Jean Marzollo
A Porcupine Named Fluffy	Helen Lester
Pest Fest	Julia Durango

Motivation Resources

Q is for Duck	Mary Elting & Michael Folsom
Rhyming Dust Bunnies	Jan Thomas
The Scrambled States of America	Laurie Keller
Shark versus Train	Chris Barton
Stephanie's Ponytail	Robert Munsch
The Stinky Cheeseman and Other Fairly Stupid Tales	Jon Scieszka
"Stand Back," Said the Elephant, "I'm Going to Sneeze."	Patricia Thomas
Stuck	Oliver Jeffers
Tacky the Penguin	Helen Lester
The Three Little Wolves and the Big Bad Pig	Eugene Trivizas
The Toughest Cowboy: or How the Wild West Was Tamed	John Frank
Waking Beauty	Leah Wilcox
Yours Truly, Goldilocks	Alma Fior Ada
There's a Zoo in Room 22	Judy Sierra

Building Better Readers

WEB-BASED RESOURCES FOR MOTIVATING READERS

Jokes, Puns, and Riddles

www.azkidsnet.com/riddles.htm

www.squiglysplayhouse.com/JokesAndRiddles

www.bestfamilyadvice.com/riddles.html

http://www.cleanjoke.com/

http://www.ahajokes.com

Funny Pictures, Signs, Headlines, etc

http://icanhascheezburger.com/

http://www.witty-quotes.com/Funny-signs/

http://funnies.paco.to/Headlines.html

http://www.witty-quotes.com/Funny-headlines/

http://www.buzzfeed.com/mjs538/the-50-funniest-headlines-of-2011

www.stephenbiesty.co.uk/galleries_main.html (This specific page is for visual learners who will enjoy all the fabulous illustrations by Stephan Biesty)

Reading Circles

www.litcircles.org

http://www.mrcoley.com/litcircles.htm

www.abcteach.com/directory/basics/reading/literature_circles/

FRACTURED FIGURATIVE LANGUAGE!

It's always darkest before................Daylight Savings Time.

Never underestimate the power of..........termites.

You can lead a horse to water but.........how?

Don't bite the hand that...................looks dirty.

No news is...............................impossible.

A miss is as good as a....................Mr.

You can't teach an old dog new............math.

Love all, trust...........................me.

The pen is mightier than the..............pigs.

An idle mind is...........................the best way to relax.

Where there's smoke there's...............pollution.

Happy is the bride who....................gets all the presents.

A penny saved is..........................not much.

Two's company, three's....................the Musketeers.

Laugh and the whole world laughs with you, cry and................you have to blow your nose.

Children should be seen and not...........spanked or grounded.

If at first you don't succeed.............get new batteries.

You get out of something what you.........see pictured on the box.

When the blind leadeth the blind..........get out of the way.

Building Better Readers

KIDS WORDS OF WISDOM
Can you explain why these are funny?

1. Never trust a dog to watch your food.

2. When your dad is mad and asks you, "Do I look stupid?" don't answer him.

3. Never tell your mom her diet's not working.

4. Stay away from prunes.

5. Never allow your three-year old brother in the same room as your school assignment.

6. Puppies still have bad breath even after eating a tic tac.

7. Never hold a dust buster and a cat at the same time.

8. You can't hide a piece of broccoli in a glass of milk.

9. If you want a kitten, start out by asking for a horse.

10. Felt markers are not good to use as lipstick.

11. Don't pick on your sister when she's holding a baseball bat.

12. Never try to baptize a cat.

Motivation Resources

JUST FOR LAUGHS QUIZ
(Great for group discussion, critical thinking, and reading fun!)

Questions

1. Is there a fourth of July in England?

2. How many birthdays does the average man have?

3. Some months have 31 days, how many have 28?

4. How many outs are there in an inning?

5. Is it legal for a man in California to marry his widow's sister?

6. Divide 30 by 1/2 and add 10. What is the answer?

7. If there are 3 apples and you take away 2, how many do you have?

8. A doctor gives you three pills telling you to take one every half hour. How many minutes would the pills last?

9. A farmer has 17 sheep, and all but 9 die. How many are left?

10. A clerk in the butcher shop is 5'10" tall. What does he weigh?

11. How many two cent stamps are there in a dozen?

12. You are participating in a race. You overtake the second person. What position are you in?

13. If you overtake the last person, then you are...?

14. Very tricky math! Note: This must be done in your head only. Do NOT use paper and pencil or a calculator. Try it: Take 1000 and add 40 to it. Now add another 1000. Now add 30. Add another 1000. Now add 20. Now add another 1000. Now add 10. What is the total?

15. Mary's father has five daughters: Nana, Nene, Nini, Nono. What is the name of the fifth daughter?

(ANSWERS START ON NEXT PAGE)

Building Better Readers

Just For Laughs Quiz Answers

1. Is there a fourth of July in England?
   Yes, it comes after the third of July!

2. How many birthdays does the average person have?
   Just one! Mine is March 24th. What's yours?

3. Some months have 31 days, how many have 28?
   Twelve - all of them have at least 28 days! (Some have a few more...)

4. How many outs are there in an inning?
   Six - three per team.

5. Is it legal for a man in California to marry his widow's sister?
   No. A widow's husband is dead – so he can't marry her sister!

6. Divide 30 by 1/2 and add 10. What is the answer?
   70 (30 divided by 2 equals 15, but 30 divided by 1/2 equals 60).

7. If there are 3 apples and you take away 2, how many do you have?
   Two. You took them, remember?

8. A doctor gives you three pills telling you to take one every half hour. How many minutes would the pills last?
   60 minutes, start with the 1st pill. 30 minutes later take the 2nd, then 30 minutes for the 3rd.

9. A farmer has 17 sheep, and all but 9 die. How many are left?
   Nine are still alive. It says so right in the question!

10. A clerk in the butcher shop is 5'10" tall. What does he weigh?
    Meat, a butcher weighs meat. That's his job!!!

11. How many two cent stamps are there in a dozen?
    There are 12 stamps in a dozen (regardless of how much they are worth).

12. You are participating in a race. You overtake the second person. What position are you in?
    If you overtake the second person and you take his place, you are second!

13. If you overtake the last person, then you are...?
    How can you overtake the LAST person? You must be the last person and you can't overtake yourself.

14. Very tricky math!
    Did you get 5000? The correct answer is actually 4100.

15. Mary's father has five daughters: Nana, Nene, Nini, Nono. What is the name of the fifth daughter?
    The fifth daughter's name is Mary. Read the question again.

Appendix

SUPPLEMENTAL INFORMATION

Building Better Readers

Appendix

INFORMAL ASSESSMENT OF LITERACY SKILLS

Let's give credit where credit is due. The resources in this section related to informal assessment of literacy have been provided by Dr. Diana Newman reviewer extraordinaire. She pointed out that informal reading inventories (IRI) are an invaluable resource for SLPs to provide the baseline data necessary for progress monitoring. It is a terrific idea and I wish I had thought of it. Unfortunately, I couldn't figure out a way to interweave this information into each chapter. Consequently, I am including her suggestions here.

IRIs are widely used to assess reading problems and understand how a student constructs meaning and uses word-attack strategies. They can provide information about students' independent, instructional, and frustration reading levels. They can also be used to determine present levels of performance related to reading fluency. IRIs consist of sets of graded word lists and passages that students read both silently and aloud. Below are some ideas for each of the key components of literacy based on the report of the National Reading Panel.

❖ NOTE: Live links for these websites can be found on the Dynamic Resources website (www.dynamic-resources.org)

COMMON CORE
SKILLS-BASED ASSESSMENT OF CORE COMMUNICATION STANDARDS: K-2
WWW.DYNAMIC-RESOURCES.ORG

PHONEMIC AWARENESS

http://teams.lacoe.edu/reading/assessments/assessments.html

Informal Assessment for:
- Recognizing Rhyme
- Isolating Beginning Sounds
- Isolating Final Sounds
- Phoneme Blending
- Yopp-Singer Test of Phonemic Segmentation

http://www.getreadytoread.org/screening-tools

- Get Ready to Read Screening Tool
- The Early Learning Observation Rating Scale (early literacy is one aspect of this informal assessment)

Building Better Readers

PHONICS

http://www.scholastic.com/content/collateral_resources/pdf/r/reading_bestpractices_phonics_nonsensewordtest.pdf

- assesses skill utilizing nonsense words (this has been found to be the best measure for decoding skill)

http://www.collingswood.k12.nj.us/ourpages/auto/2009/10/29/36702151/Basic%20Phonics%20Assessment_doc.pdf

- assesses decoding using real words

READING FLUENCY

http://www.mrsperkins.com/dolch.htm

- Dolch (sight) words by grade

http://www.readingrockets.org/article/31295/

- Normative charts for Words Correct Per Minute [wcpm].

VOCABULARY

http://www.readingrockets.org/article/41555/

- Classroom Vocabulary Assessment for Content Areas

COMPREHENSION:

http://www.interventioncentral.org/tools/maze-passage-generator

- Times measures of reading comprehension using a maze generator. Can be administered to an entire class or a single student.

http://www.studentprogress.org/summer_institute/2007/Intro%20reading/IntroReading_Manual_2007.pdf

- On-line manual for using Curriculum Based Measurement for Progress Monitoring in Reading (Fuchs & Fuchs, 2003)

Appendix

REFERENCES AND RECOMMENDED READING

Adams, M. (1995). Beginning to read: Thinking and learning about print. Cambridge, MA: MIT Press.

Adams, M. (1992) Phoneme awareness is a better predictor of early reading skill than onset-rime awareness Journal of Experimental Child Psychology 31:1, 2-28.

Apel, K., Masterson, J.J., & Wilson-Fowler, E.B. (2011). Developing word-level literacy skills in children with and without typical communication skills. In S. Ellis, E. McCartney, & J. Bourne (Eds.), Insight and impact: Applied linguistics and the primary school. (pp. 229-241). London, UK: Cambridge University Press.

Armbruster, B., Lehr, F., & Osborn, J. (2001). Put reading first:The research building blocks for teaching children to read. Jessup, MD: National Institute for Literacy.

Baumann, J.F., Ware, D., & Edwards, E.C. (2007). "Bumping into spicy, tasty words that catch your tongue:" A formative experiment on vocabulary instruction. The Reading Teacher, 61(2), 108-122.

Beck, I., McKeown, M., & Kucan, L. (2002). Bringing Words to Life: Robust Vocabulary Instruction. Guildford Press.

Biemiller, A. (2005). Size and sequence in vocabulary development: Implications for choosing words for primary grade vocabulary instruction. In A. Hiebert & M. Kamil, (Eds.), Teaching and learning vocabulary: Bringing research to practice (pp. 223-242). Mahwah, NJ: Erlbaum.

Bishop, A., Yopp, R. & Yopp, H (2000). Ready for reading: A handbook for parents of preschoolers. Boston: Allyn and Bacon.

Catts, H., Fey, M., & Tomlin, B. (2002). A longitudinal investigation of reading outcomes in children with language impairments. Journal of Speech and Hearing Research, 45, 1142-1157.

Catts, H. & Kamhi A. (1999). Language and reading disabilities. Boston, MA: Allyn & Bacon.

Chard, D., Vaughn, S., & Tyler, B. (2002). A synthesis of research on effective interventions for building reading fluency with elementary students with learning disabilities. Journal of Learning Disabilities, 35, 386–407.

Graves, M. F. (2000). A vocabulary program to complement and bolster a middle-grade comprehension program. In B. Taylor, M. F. Graves, and P. van den Broek (Eds.), Reading for meaning: Fostering comprehension in the middle grades (pp. 116-135). New York: Teachers College Press.

Graves, M.F. (2006). The vocabulary book: Learning and instruction. New York: Teachers College Press.

Graves, M. Beck, Isabel L., McKeown, Margaret G., & Kucan, Linda. (2002). Bringing words to life. New York, NY: The Guilford Press.

Hayes, D. P., & Ahrens, M. (1988). Vocabulary simplification for children: A special case of 'motherese.' Journal of Child Language, 15, 395-410. Hiebert, E.H. & Kamil, M. (Eds.) (2005), Teaching and learning vocabulary: Bringing scientific research to practice. Mahwah, NJ: Erlbaum.

National Institute of Child Health and Human Development. (2000). Report of the National Reading Panel. Teaching children to read: an evidence-based assessment of the scientific research literature on reading and its implications for reading instruction.

Available at: http://www.nichd.nih.gov/publications/nrp/smallbook.htm.

McKeown, M. G., & Beck, I. L. (2003). Taking advantage of read-alouds to help children make sense of decontextualized language. In A. van Kleeck, S. Stahl, & E. Bauer (Eds.), On reading books to children (pp. 159-176). Mahwah, NJ: Erlbaum.

McKeown, M. G., Beck, I. L., Omanson, R. C., & Pople, M. T. (1985). Some effects of the nature and frequency of vocabulary instruction on the knowledge and use of words. Reading Research Quarterly, 20, 522-535.

Montgomery, Judy K. (2006). The bridge of vocabulary: Evidence-based activities for academic success. San Antonio: Pearson.

Montogmery, J. & Kahn, N. (2003). You are going to be an author: Using narrative for adolescent language intervention. Communication Disorders Quarterly, 24,5.

Appendix

Snow, C. E., Tabors, P. O., Nicholson, P. A., & Kurland, B. F. (1995). SHELL: Oral language and early literacy skills in kindergarten and first grade children. Journal of Research in Childhood Education, 10, 37-48.

Snowling, M. (2005). Phonological processing and developmental dyslexia. Journal of Research in Reading,18, 132-138.

Stahl, S. A. (1999). Vocabulary development. Cambridge, MA: Brookline Books.

Stahl, S. A., & Nagy, W. E. (2000). Promoting vocabulary development. Austin: Texas Education Agency.

Stothard, S. E., Snowling, M. J., Bishop, D. V. M.,Chipchase, B. B., & Kaplan, C. A. (1998). Language impaired preschoolers: A follow-up into adolescence. Journal of Speech, Language, and Hearing Research, 41,407–418.

Wasowicz, J., Apel, K., Masterson, J. & Whitney, A. (2012) SPELL-Links to Reading & Writing: A Word-Study Curriculum (2nd edition). Evanston, IL: Learning By Design, Inc. www.learningbydesign.com

Weizman, Z.O., & Snow, C.E. (2001). Lexical input as related to children's vocabulary acquisition: Effects of sophisticated exposure and support for meaning.Developmental Psychology, 37, 265-279.

Yopp, H. & Yopp, R. (200)0. Supporting phonemic awareness development in the classroom. The Reading Teacher, 54,130-143.